LITTLE FREE LIBRARY
ALWAYS FREE
NEVER FOR SALE

NOT-SO-SECRET SECRETS
The No Nonsense Aboveground Playbook
by Brandon Hofer

LITTLE FREE LIBRARY
ALWAYS FREE
NEVER FOR SALE

NOT-SO-SECRET SECRETS: The No Nonsense Aboveground Playbook

Copyright © 2020 by Brandon Hofer

All rights reserved. No part of this book may be reproduced in any form on by an electronic or mechanical means, including information storage and retrieval systems, without permission in writing from the publisher, except by a reviewer who may quote brief passages in a review.

ISBN 978-1-71688-238-8

TABLE OF CONTENTS

FOREWARD: NIC PETERSON 1
INTRODUCTION - DON'T GET HELD HOSTAGE 5
PHASE 1 - SOLID FOUNDATIONS 8
   CHAPTER 1 - YOUR UNIQUE EXPERTISE 10
      DISCOVER YOUR SUPERPOWERS 13
   CHAPTER 2 - THE ENTREPRENEUR'S MINDSET 20
      THE SHIFT 23
      MIND-SHIFT ACTION STEP 25
   CHAPTER 3 - A LIFE BY DESIGN 28
      THE NON-NEGOTIABLES 30
      LIFE BY DESIGN ACTION STEP 34
      THE PERFECT DAY 35
PHASE 2 - DESIGNING THE MONEY-MAKER 36
   CHAPTER 4 - COMMITTING TO THE PATH 38
      IDEAL CLIENT 44
   CHAPTER 5 - THE HEART OF YOUR BRAND 46
      UNDERSTAND THEIR LEVEL OF AWARENESS 47
      GET CONCRETE AND GRANULAR 49
      TELL STORIES OF PEOPLE LIKE THEM 52
      GETTING CLARITY 54
   CHAPTER 6 - CRAFTING YOUR IRRESISTIBLE OFFERS 56
      THE PREMIUM OFFER 58
      THE LEVERAGED OFFER 61
      THE AUTOMATED PROGRAM 63
      YOUR PROGRAM PROCESS 66

PHASE 3 - ONLINE GROWTH 68
CHAPTER 7 - BUILDING YOUR TRIBE 69
- THE FACEBOOK TRIFECTA 70
- THE COCKTAIL PARTY 74

CHAPTER 8 - VALUE DRIVEN ENROLLMENT 78
- THE SESSION BY SESSION STRUGGLE... 80
- SALES MASTERY... 83

CHAPTER 9 - RISING ABOVE THE NOISE 90
- ATTRACTION 92
- CONNECTION 93
- RETENTION 95
- PERFECTION 96

PHASE 4 - THE RIGHT TOOLS FOR THE JOB 98
CHAPTER 10 - EVERYTHING YOU NEED TO GROW 100
- SIMPLIFIED ORGANIZATION 101
- VIDEO HOSTING 101
- SCREEN RECORDING SOFTWARE 102
- SLIDE CREATION SOFTWARE... 103
- BUSINESS BANK ACCOUNT 104
- ALL THE REST 105

CHAPTER 11 - ELIMINATING UNNECESSARY QUESTIONS 107
- WHICH TOOL IS "BEST?" 108
- WHAT WILL I PUT IN MY PROGRAM? 109
- WHICH TACTIC IS "BEST?" 111

CHAPTER 12 - ACTION AND MOMENTUM 113
- BUILDING THE AUTOMATION 115
- ONGOING GROWTH 118

PHASE 5 - THE P.L.A.N. METHOD TO MULTIPLY PROFITS 121

CHAPTER 13 - LAYERING VALUE **123**
   THE LEVERAGED FULFILLMENT MODEL 125
   PUTTING IT IN PLAY 130
CHAPTER 14 - CREATING STABILITY **131**
   STABILITY THROUGH AUDIENCE GROWTH 135
   DESIGNING THE AUTOMATED OFFER 137
CHAPTER 15 - OPTIMIZING FOR CLIENT RESULTS **139**
   CLEAR INSTRUCTIONS AFTER PURCHASE 140
   CLIENT AMPLIFIERS 144
NEVER DONE 148
WHAT'S NEXT AND ACTION ITEMS 149

FOREWARD: NIC PETERSON

Another book about online business? Really? Isn't the internet marketing and online business world complicated enough, with enough information to drown us all already?

There was a time when information was valuable. Having useful information was like having a specific plant in the middle of a desert. Times have changed, information is everywhere and, by and large, it's free. The internet has brought us infinite opportunity in how we run our business and design our lives, but it has changed the value of information.

What we need, now more than ever, is not more stuff to do or information to take in. What used to be a desert is now a rainforest *- and the greatest value to someone is helping them pinpoint a very specific plant in an overly crowded rainforest.*

Success in the internet age is about knowing where to look, but more importantly, knowing what to ignore.

What I love most about business owners like Brandon, that have been successful over a long period of time in fitness, is that they understand the importance of the right thing at the right time (sequence) and playing the long game.

Not-So-Secret Secrets is appropriately named because what Brandon breaks down is fundamental, but often ignored.

Things like...

- Long term consequences of short term wins
- Optimizing for the right thing
- Getting closer to the life that you want
- Making sure you're winning a race you actually want to be in

And it all has an underpinning of fundamentals that actually work.

How do you learn how things actually work?

With a deep reverence for all that has come before it.

If you're online, study what has worked offline. If you're offline, study what has worked online...But also by making friends with the eminent dead.

Tracing the genealogy of your business/field all the way to its roots, it's founders and it's innovators.

Anything less leaves you skating on intellectual razor thin ice.

What has tempted will always tempt and what has motivated will always motivate.

Basically, human nature hasn't changed.

For this reason, attempts at invention or innovation in marketing, advertising, selling or building a culture is frivolous at best.

There is no "new way" to sell $50k in business with a two step funnel. There never will be.

Big, sustainable business success is derived from fundamental principles determining or governing strategy.

Principles that are, by and large, preference based.

Then, the preference based strategy determines governing tactics.

There is no room for cookie cutter advice when reasoning from the ground up.

What most marketing "gurus" realize (and then sell you) quickly is that you can gain a lot of speed by jumping directly to tactics.

Build a webinar!
Raise your price!
Use this sales script!
Nonsense.

Foolish behavior encouraged by the internet, immediate gratification, Alexa, and Google.

.....and, of course, people in a similar position as you trying to build a foundation by selling the lack of one to you.

Well, my friend.

You are in luck.

The people in my world, like Brandon, won't let you skate on thin ice.

If you're ready (and eager) to build a business online that is robust and will serve you and your family for a very long time... read on.

Nic Peterson

To connect further with Nic Peterson, and get his new book Customers for Life, go here:

https://earncustomersforlife.com

Brandon Hofer

INTRODUCTION - DON'T GET HELD HOSTAGE

Imagine waking up one day and being told that your entire business must be shut down because of a variable you are not in control of. That's exactly what happened to me, and it was the catalyst that forcefully pushed me to finally take the leap I had been considering for years - create an online coaching business and embrace full responsibility for my life, my family, and my income.

After 10 years in the fitness industry, I had done it all - Personal Trainer, Fitness Manager, Area Director of Fitness, Gym Owner, and Independent Fitness Coach. When working as a Fitness Coach, training people at a local area gym, life was okay-ish. I was fully booked, but actually quite miserable. "6-figures" wasn't really working out for me because it meant long work weeks, split shifts, and missing way too much family time with my wife and two daughters.

Have you ever had a gut instinct that you know you want more out of life? Deep down, you have an urge to break free from your current life situation and grow beyond your circumstance. I had that urge, but it wasn't until we got the news of the gym shutting down that I was forced to make that life-altering decision.

The gym I was training out of at the time was not mine. Myself and a few other coaches were simply renting space to train our clients.

When we got the news that it would be shutting down completely, everyone had 2 weeks to make a new plan.

It was exhausting thinking about having to uproot my business and start again at another physical location, so I made a firm decision to intentionally level up and create a new reality for myself.

I referred every single fitness client to my colleagues in the area that I trusted and made a clean break. I would create an online coaching business and never again be held hostage by anyone else or their business.

I immediately went to work as a sales rep for a home remodel company to pay the bills as I began laying the foundation for what would eventually become The Online Coach Creator, a business that helps you make the same transition I did - monetizing your expert skill set with an online business.

It's one of the hottest topics right now, and for good reason. Billions of dollars are being made by entrepreneurs worldwide who leverage their wisdom, expertise, life experience, and counsel to build thriving businesses and earn whatever they desire.

Looking back on the journey now, I only wish I had started sooner.

I wrote this book to help you get started on this journey.

As the title suggests, these aren't the super secret "underground" tips and tricks that everyone else promotes. In these pages, you'll find tried and true business building principles applied to the context of online service-based business.

It's not a secret. It's not a magic pill. And it's definitely not how to become a millionaire in a few short weeks with minimal effort.

Instead, it's about creating a life that you want and generating new depths of joy, satisfaction, connection, and gratitude.

And ultimately, it's about leaving a legacy, so you don't wake up one day wishing you had started 10 years ago.

So now it's time - make the decision. Choose to begin. And if you're ready to take this gig seriously, I'm here for you. And together, we'll build your dream.

PHASE 1
SOLID FOUNDATIONS

Usually when we talk about creating new opportunities in life through an online business, everyone wants to skip ahead to the sexy stuff like marketing and profit. But you don't get a dream lifestyle by skipping ahead and ignoring the fundamentals.

Solid Foundations ask you to look inward first, before you go about creating something external. It's acknowledging that finding a connection to yourself and your ideal life will be the driving motivational force behind everything else that you do.
I don't believe that anyone wants to build a business if it means they have to sacrifice the rest of their life in order to make that business happen.

At least, that's not what I want. And if you've got the entrepreneurial itch, my guess is it's because you want it all! Amazing life, profitable business, vibrant health, satisfying relationships, and a sense of peace to replace that biting existential anxiety we start to feel when we know we're not aligned with what we're meant to do in this life.

If that's you, I encourage you to charge ahead and consume this book quickly so you can create a plan and start taking action on it as soon as possible.

Fortune favors the bold. But that doesn't mean you shouldn't equip yourself first before you dive into the great unknown.

CHAPTER 1
YOUR UNIQUE EXPERTISE

I think we all have an intuitive sense, deep down, that we have something unique and special to offer this world. We might not think about it consciously on a regular basis, but it's there. We might get glimpses of it on occasion before we get caught up again in the day to day hustle bustle of trying to make a living and navigate the intricacies of life, but it never really disappears.

Ever since I can remember remembering things, I've always felt that I am here to make a difference. And yeah, I know that sounds kinda vague, but for the last 38 years I've been trying to piece together what that actually means and how I might order the rest of my life around that feeling that I'm called to do something truly meaningful with my life.

I'm willing to bet that you've felt this feeling too. And ultimately, that's what this book is about. And sure, I'm gonna give you some really great actionable stuff to do to build your business, but if we can't stay connected to this deeper driving force, then all the other stuff won't matter.

So before we get into the details of business strategies, tactics, program design, and then marketing and selling your new online coaching program, we must first dig into the reason you've chosen this type of client-based business as a calling and business venture in the first place.

There is a reason you feel compelled to offer the specific service that you are offering, and in my experience, this is always related to your personal story and what I call your Unique Expertise.

Here's the thing - No one else has the blend of raw talent and abilities, combined with life experience, that you do. And when you tap into that power, you will be unstoppable.

When you reconnect with your innate desires and your unique talents, which develop because you've been naturally drawn to them your whole life, you will unleash your unique superpower on the world.

There's a scene from the 2017 movie Wonder Woman, where they are trying to cross "No Man's Land" and Diana is trying to convince her companion, Steve Trevor, that they have to cross the battlefield to help the villagers on the other side. Steve tells Diana that they can't help the villagers because they can't save everyone and that "this is not what we came here to do."

Diana then places her Wonder Woman crest on her forehead and says, "No, but it's what *I'm* going to do." She then removes her outer coat, revealing her shield and full battle gear as she climbs the ladder out of the trench and walks straight into enemy fire. And then of course the epic background music starts playing as she finally reveals her superpowers for all to see and leads the team across No Man's Land so they can all save the villagers!

This scene always gives me goosebumps. Partially because deflecting bullets with golden gauntlets is really cool, and partially because I'm a Dad to two amazing daughters, and I want them to grow up to be badass superheroes too! But beyond that, deep down, there is something about this scene that resonates with all of us.

We all have that superpower, buried under the outer coat, and we have people around us telling us, "Don't do that. That's not what we came here to do." And somewhere deep down you're thinking, "No, but it's what I came here to do! And I *am* going to do it!"

We know intuitively within our soul that we are given certain gifts at birth, and it's up to us to cultivate those gifts so that they become true strengths and can then be used to help someone else in this life.

This is the place to begin this journey because unless you are connected to your greater purpose, you'll either give up before your business has a chance to flourish, or you'll build an incredible business and look back at it 2 years from now and wish that you hadn't built it! And working hard to build something that you will ultimately not want is worse than a failed business.

Think about it. When you do something because you feel compelled to by someone else, or it doesn't resonate with you on a gut level, that thing always turns out mediocre. But when you are actively engaged in a life pursuit that you know you are meant for, then you'll willingly work 10x harder at it because it feels effortless.

So the next obvious question is how do you discover your superpower, and how can you apply it to your new business venture.

Let me give you one exercise that I do with my clients at our live retreats that I think is the best way to get in touch with your raw superpower so you can start living in it right away

DISCOVER YOUR SUPERPOWERS

This process has two main parts. First, I highly recommend that you buy the StrengthsFinder book and take the online assessment included. I don't work for these folks and I'm not even certified through them, I have just found more value taking their assessment than every other personality profile assessment tool I've ever experienced, and so I recommend it to everyone I know.

You'll receive a breakdown of your Top 5 Strengths and an explanation of how each one works. This will be the foundation of selecting your True Identity Symbol.

Next, you'll write down your Top 5 Strengths on a sheet of paper with space between each one, so you have room to do some self-reflection and journaling.

Write down HOW you can exercise each of those strengths on a daily basis. For example, one of my Top 5 Strengths is what they call Learner. It simply means that acquiring new skills and knowledge naturally fires me up and I'm at my best when I'm learning something new. When I got my assessment back, this immediately resonated with me because I used to think that there was something wrong with me since I got bored with doing the same thing over and over. I thought, "oh, I can't stick with something long term, I must not have the discipline of commitment." But when I started living within my Learner Strength, I could all of a sudden stick with a project indefinitely, I just had to also be engaged actively with learning as I was doing it, and then the commitment piece came easily.

I use this on a daily basis, because now I schedule in time to learn something new or acquire a new skill and as long as I do that, I'm able to stay committed to other projects long term.

Now it's your turn. Write them down. Yes, actually write them down.

Then start journaling how you can use each one in your daily activities. You'll be shocked at our practical and relevant this simple exercise is when it comes to laying the foundation for a high impact and profitable online business.

Now the second part. After you've written down the practical application of your strengths, it's time to select your True Identity Symbol. This is a metaphorical image that you connect with, that highlights key aspects of your character or desired daily activities. This can be an existing person, fictional or real, and it can also be a symbol or image. Or it can be a little of both.

Here are a few examples. Let's say you admire the idea of Batman (yes, I just seriously suggested that you can be Batman if you want to be). You admire that he is very intelligent, a clever detective, physically strong, action-oriented, and that he lives for a cause higher than himself. See how this works?

Or it could be a real person. Perhaps you admire Abraham Lincoln because of his dedication to his cause, his patience, and the way he exemplified leadership during a time period of intense conflict in the United States.

The idea here is that you get to pick who (or what) you want to be, and you can combine all of their characteristics, or just the ones you resonate with. Maybe you want to be James Bond + Mother Teresa because your ideal image of yourself includes the suave, cool nature of an undercover spy, but you also want to emulate the unconditional love of Mother Teresa.

I have one client who says that she feels like a cross between Ellen and David Goggins! The charm, charisma, and friendly spirit of Ellen combined with the no nonsense "just-fucking-do-the-work" approach of David Goggins would certainly make for a phenomenal character blend.

For those of you familiar with the writing of Napoleon Hill, you may recognize this as a version of what he writes about in the Law of Success book. For Hill, he would create vivid imaginary meetings in his mind with historical figures and ask them how he might emulate their positive qualities and integrate them with his own life.

The idea here is that when you activate your imagination and envision who you want to become, your subconscious mind goes to work and helps you reshape your identity to become more and more like who you desire to be.

Let's go even deeper now. Pick a symbol or collection of symbols that resonate with you. For me, one symbol that has always struck a heart-cord with me is a sword. In many ancient texts and scriptures, the sword was a symbol of the spoken word, and very often used to designate a message from a divine source that was meant to inspire and encourage the world. That symbol resonates with me because I know that part of my mission on this Earth is to be speaking from stages and encouraging people as I help them create freedom in their life, especially by creating new businesses and income sources for themselves.

And if I wanted to, I could also adopt the sword imagery to be part of my writing activity. I could say that the words of encouragement and education that I want to give to the world need not be limited to speaking from stage, but could also be written, and even in audio recording or video form. The point here is that while there are loose guidelines to this exercise, you have a lot of room to play around and exercise creativity.

While working through this exercise, a friend of mine said he wanted to be the image of a tree. I asked him what it was about the tree that he felt exemplified his mission. He told me that the tree had a strong foundation in its root system, but then grew up tall and strong and spread its branches all over. Part of the vision he had for his life was to be someone with a firm foundation who would then reach out to help other people, no matter where he lived or what task he had before him.

The symbol you choose for yourself need not be static. That's the power of metaphor: It can change and adapt as you grow and as your opportunities and context change over time.

Okay, so what could this look like if you put it all together? What happens when you combine your True Identity Symbol with your Strengths to unleash your Unique Expertise?

You'll have a blueprint for who you are, which shapes how you look at every new opportunity that comes your way. It will also shape which activities you focus on each day, because you'll naturally be drawn to the actions that reinforce your Unique Expertise.

Wanna start a business that helps other people lose over 100 lbs and get their health and life back? Great! Now take the assessment to reveal your Top 5 Strengths, and then you'll be able to apply each strength to whatever coaching or training program you create. Then you might say, for example, that you want to be the Yoda of weight loss because Yoda is always dropping wisdom bombs and helping people rethink their own perspective.

Did you spend over 20 years as a CEO helping turn around failing businesses, and now you want to teach the next generation that same skill so they can contribute to the health of the economy? Perfect! Which of your Top 5 Strengths will you use most often? And which person or alter-ego do you identify with? Maybe Morpheus from the movie The Matrix because he is a wise teacher who shows Neo the path. Or maybe you prefer Maui from the movie Moana because he helps the heroine discover her own unique skills that eventually lead to them saving their island home and restoring the heart of their tribe.

The point here is that you are not just a letter on a DISC profile, or a combination of letters from a Meyers-Briggs assessment, or even a number from an Enneagram test. You are a distinct blend of raw talent, specific strengths, unique life experience, and deep connection with icons and examples from history, even if those characters are fictional.

And when you take the time to reflect on all these variables and start to look around you for characters and metaphors that you identify with, you will get closer and closer each day to both your Unique Expertise and your True Purpose and Calling. As you get closer and closer to your True Purpose, you'll find more and more satisfaction with your life situation, which transforms your Mid-Life Crisis into a Mid-Life Rebirth.

But that's a topic for another book. Fow now, let's get back to launching that online business you've been dreaming of.

CHAPTER 2
THE ENTREPRENEUR'S MINDSET

Back when I was a personal trainer at the local big box gym, part of the initial client assessment involved discussing nutrition. I learned very quickly that I had to ask people specific questions like "what did you eat for breakfast yesterday?" to get accurate information. If I used a broader question like, "how's your nutrition?" people would always answer "well, I eat pretty healthy" even though they actually had a bagel with cream cheese and a mocha for breakfast yesterday.

In a similar vein, I can't tell you how many times I've heard entrepreneurs say "my mindset is great, I've got that dialed in," when their reality was quite the opposite.

Let me explain.

Your daily schedule, your programs and offers, your enrollment percentage, your organic marketing content, and your entire business is a reflection of your mindset. And look, I know there are entire books and seminars written on this single topic, so we don't need to hash out every last little detail in this chapter.
Instead, I'd like to show the one mind-shift that will have the deepest and most immediate impact on your business.

If you're thinking right now that perhaps you can skip this chapter and get right to the "real" information, or that you've already sorted out your mindset, then that is proof positive that you need this chapter more than ever!

If someone told me, "oh, yeah, Brandon I did a few workouts last year, so my fitness is totally dialed in," I'd roll my eyes and help them find the nearest kettlebell because we'd have work to do my friend!

Instinctively, we know that health, wealth, relationships, business, creativity, and every other worthwhile pursuit is the accumulation of our habit patterns rather than a one time action. So why would mindset be any different?

The process of rewiring your brain is not a one-and-done endeavour. It's a lifetime pursuit to condition yourself with thoughts and feelings that energize you and spread that positive energy to those around you.

The fancy term for this is the "aggregation of marginal gains," which simply means that tiny incremental practices implemented on a daily basis produce fractional and barely distinguishable gains in the moment, but over time the compound effect of these marginal gains produces monumental results!

Two beers with dinner isn't a big deal that day. But two beers with dinner every night for 5 years will give you a nice round tummy and probably stunt your creative growth.

And on the flip side, a 10-minute affirmation with positive thought might help you feel better for a few minutes that day, but a 10-minute affirmation with positive thought every day for 5 years can literally transform everything about your personality and life!

And while we're on the topic of affirmations, be sure to check out our YouTube Channel, "Online Success for Coaches" and subscribe for more awesome business training as well as a vault full of simple but powerful affirmations that you can use to create new realities in your life.

So anyway, here's what I'm getting at - Mindset work is never done, the same way that health is never done or completely sorted out. It's a lifelong pursuit.

So in light of that truth, what's the one mind-shift that you can actively pursue right now that will influence every facet of your business from the beginning so you don't inadvertently sabotage your results before you even make your first sale?

You have to make the shift from an Employee Mindset to an Entrepreneur's Mindset to succeed in this game long term.

This means you will view Time, Money, Accountability, and Client Experience in the exact opposite way that you have up until this shift.

THE SHIFT

An employee typically gets paid hourly or a salary, sometimes with incentive possibilities. Someone else determines what they should do each day, and they are accountable only to show up for the designated time slot, put the effort in, and then they receive compensation. Notwithstanding gross incompetence, that employee is rarely held to a higher standard of accountability. Even in a service-based industry, like personal training, accountability is still determined by simply showing up and helping someone workout. When I had clients who paid for me to help them lose weight, or reduce stress, or gain strength, or whatever their goal was, I got paid to be physically present whether they binged on pizza and oreos every night or not.

Even if you're a business owner, if you're still operating primarily on a session by session model, or an hourly model, you're still at least partially connected to the employee mindset. Just because you no longer have a boss doesn't mean you've made the full mind-shift yet! And staying connected to the employee mindset will kill your long term growth faster than anything else.

When you assume that the value you bring, and thus the price you charge, is only as good as your direct involvement, then you'll never be able to break free into full Entrepreneur Mode, where you can build systems that create outcomes, and then you simply oversee the application of those systems into the lives or businesses of those you serve. Can you see the difference?

It means you become a leader while still helping other people get the same result that you helped them get when you provided nothing but one-on-one sessions or done-for-you services.

The transition out of this Employee paradigm is to fully embrace your new role as someone who designs transformational programs for people, which we'll cover in detail in Phase 2 of this book. You'll see step by step how to do this so you can actually guarantee your clients' success with full integrity.

And when you sell based on outcomes and life transitions rather than sessions, both you and your clients are finally free to do your best work together, and you can break out of the Employee Mindset and start crafting offers that are high impact, high value, and challenge you to become a better and better service provider every single day.

If you ever find yourself slipping back into Employee Mindset mode, which is usually when you're tempted to just go through the motions rather than showing up fully present and attentive for your clients, you can run through some really simple reminders of the truth:

You are a powerful creator in your own life. You are fully capable to guide those you serve through a process of real change with your predictable process. You have every resource you need right now to make powerful steps forward in your business. You are completely qualified to serve your clients, and they are happy to pay you a premium rate because you always deliver the highest quality service with real outcomes.

So before we move on, I want to give you one very simple and straightforward action step you can implement immediately that will cultivate the Entrepreneur's Mindset within.

Now, I have to warn you, this action step operates on the same premise as a quality fitness plan or nutrition program. It's based on the aggregation of marginal gains. You don't do it once and then pat yourself on the back while claiming you've "got that Mindset thing all sorted out."

Instead, you must come back to this on a daily basis to remind yourself of your new identity as a powerful entrepreneur and not simply an employee who works their entire life to build someone else's business.

MIND-SHIFT ACTION STEP

After some time in quiet self-reflection in light of your new awareness of your Unique Expertise, use the space below to write down your Big Why.

In other words, think about why you want to launch this business. What is the bigger picture mission underneath it all? What is the driving force that will keep you going when things get tough or when you come across unexpected obstacles that are out of your direct control?

And it doesn't have to be just one thing. It can be a combination. Let me give you an example from my own life.

For me, my family has always been a huge motivating factor for why I initially made the leap to creating my own online client-centered business. But along with that motivation, to provide for them and live my life with a flexible schedule, is the drive to become a Freedom Fighter for other people too.

My Big Why is that I want to spread the truth that no one has to be held hostage by someone else's business or decisions ever again. So when things get challenging or I'm forced into a season of growth or adaptation that feels uncomfortable, or when I'm tempted to think it would be somehow "easier" to just get a job, I remind myself that I'm not doing this just for myself. Instead, I'm doing this to show others the way to becoming Freedom Fighters for their own lives as well.

My deeper mission here is to build a tribe of Freedom Fighters so that together we can build your dream and make sure that you are in control of your time, your income, and your relationships. In other words, to help everyone see the truth that you are a powerful creator in your own life and the only variable you're faced with each day is whether or not you choose to show up, do your best, and continue to grow.

MY BIG "WHY"

Write as much detail as you can about the deeper mission behind your business.

I do what I do because....

CHAPTER 3
A LIFE BY DESIGN

"If you refuse to create the future you want, you must settle for the future you get."

I'm convinced that no one wants to build a profitable business if it means they have to sacrifice the quality of the rest of their life in the process. At least, I know I don't! And yeah, I'm sure there are people who have done this before - built a business that generates money, but they lost their health or their families or both along the way. But I don't believe that's what they truly wanted. I believe that they simply failed to intentionally plan what they wanted their life to look like before they jumped ahead and launched the business.

I made this mistake once. And it only took once to learn my lesson and scrap the one business in order to build the one I actually wanted.

At one point, I made the transition away from working for a large corporate gym as the Area Director of Fitness and opted to create my own Personal Training business. At the time, although I had the entrepreneurial itch, I hadn't yet made the full evolution into the Entrepreneurial Mindset. As a result, I found myself in a position where I was fully booked and miserable.

When I launched my Personal Training business, I had nearly 10 years of experience in the fitness industry, so I was no stranger to the hustle it takes to build a client-centered business. Marketing and sales were familiar and I had some past clients that I could reach out to as well.

After about 3 months I had filled my schedule with clients. But they were mostly 1:1 clients, with a few small groups and workshops thrown in the mix. But in the fitness industry, filling your schedule often means accommodating people's schedules, and that means sometimes 5am sessions, sometimes 7pm sessions, and sometimes split shifts that start at 5am and end at 8pm with an awkward gap in the middle of the day.

Now, I could claim I built a "6-figure" business because I was averaging around $8,500/month in gross revenue as a solopreneur. But when I accounted for expenses, taxes, and the effect this business was having on my actual life, I realized it just wasn't worth it!

And so after grinding hard for a few more months, I finally decided to pack it up and make a firm decision to build a business online. Like many of you, I had been "thinking about it" for awhile, but just never made the leap.

"It's not the right time," I thought. "I don't know enough yet," went the repeating message in my mind. "I'm not even sure where to begin," said my recurring excuse patterns.

But we all eventually get to that breaking point, where we simply can't continue with the way things are because it's too painful and the prospect of a new life is too inspiring to keep saying no.

So what I want to help you see in this chapter, is that you can absolutely have a successful and profitable online business while at the same time creating a life by design.

When I made the leap to online coaching, I finally had enough wisdom to take the time to decide what I wanted my life to look like BEFORE I designed the model of client fulfillment that I use today.

THE NON-NEGOTIABLES

The first step to creating your life by design is to decide what your non-negotiables are. In other words, what will you gladly accept in your life and what will you no longer tolerate.

That way, most of the major choices you'll be faced with have already been decided ahead of time. Now you'll know with crystal clear clarity what you should or shouldn't do based on your own pre-established criteria.

For example, many years ago, I made a firm commitment to no longer tolerate being disrespected by a boss. That commitment led to me leaving a few jobs that were actually quite lucrative, but making me miserable because I was violating my own standards that I had set for myself.

When I laid aside my personal training business (which was also the result of abiding by a non-negotiable), I ended up in a transition zone between one business and the next. In that short season, I picked up a job selling home remodel projects for a general contractor. The pay was good as it was commission based sales, but about 6 months into it, I felt the pull of two of my non-negotiables. First, I felt my standard of not tolerating disrespect being violated, and at the same time, I was not honoring my desire to have the freedom to create my own schedule.

So I left. Simple as that. In effect, I had already made the decision ahead of time.

Am I telling you to quit your job today, throw caution to the wind, and launch your business? Maybe. But maybe not.

I'm suggesting that you first get really clear on what you will no longer tolerate in your life and then decide on what your non-negotiables are so that you have a guiding light to help you make those decisions.

Maybe, like me, you are working late into the night and you'd rather be at home with your family in the evening.

Maybe you'd like your mornings to yourself to exercise, meditate, and write that book you've been dreaming of.

Maybe you prefer to travel the world and you need an income source that accommodates that lifestyle.

Perhaps you want to work 3 hours a day, make $60,000 a year, and surf the rest of the day. Great! Let's find a way to earn that money with that schedule so you can live the lifestyle that you actually want!

Some people want to become lavishly wealthy. Others simply don't care about the money as long as their basic needs are covered and they can spend time with the people they truly care about.

When I launched my online coaching business, I made a firm decision that I would never have more than three coaching sessions per day. So I created a schedule that accommodated that desire, and then I priced my programs appropriately so that I could still meet my income goals.

Can you see how all this blends together?

The reason most online entrepreneurs fail is not because they don't have an audience of 100,000 people, and not because they don't know how to run Facebook ads, and not because they lack a marketable skill set.

Instead, it's because they never took the time to get clear on what they want and why they want it.

Your brain functions like a Google search bar. When you ask it a question, it will look for the answer to that question. So if you ask it "why isn't this working?" you'll find a bunch of reasons why your business isn't working. If you ask it "how do I get more clients?" you'll find a bunch of ideas on how to get "more" clients... which might be just one more client, since that is certainly more than you have now. But if you ask it questions like "what are my options to earn $80,000 in the next 12 months while working 6 hours a day and at the same time preserving mornings to focus on writing and evenings with my family?" Then guess what! You will start seeking that exact answer.

And you *will* find it, as long as you're willing to show up consistently and search for the answer.

And sure, you might need some support from a coach along the way to help you sift through all those thoughts in your mind that keep going around in circles and never get you anywhere. But chances are your coach will push you to define what it is that you are actually after before recommending a course of action.

LIFE BY DESIGN ACTION STEP

Here's your next step. In the space below, write down your top 5 non-negotiables. These can be things you absolutely want in your life or they can be the things you will not tolerate under any circumstances.

My Top 5 Non-Negotiables

1.

2.

3.

4.

5.

THE PERFECT DAY

Next, write down in as much detail as possible, what your perfect day would look like. Dream about your business integrated into that day as well, where everything is perfectly in place. This would be like saying, what will your life look like 5 years from now if you get started today and start intentionally creating the life you truly want.

My Perfect Day

PHASE 2
DESIGNING THE MONEY-MAKER

Now that you've gotten incredibly clear on what you want your life to look like, it's time to create valuable and irresistible offers so you can turn your passion and expertise into a profitable and sustainable business.

In Phase 2, I'll walk you through the steps to creating your very first program offer. And although I'll share examples from the realm of coaching specifically, because this is a principled based approach, it will work for any service-driven client-centered business.

One of the main threads that runs throughout the next few Phases is that you are intentionally creating outcomes for your target market, but you are selling them on the vision of what their future will look like after they work with you.

This is what separates a business like this with so many other types of business. You must become skillful at helping someone see a vision for what their life will look like in the future. Otherwise, they have no incentive to work with you, paid or otherwise.

Along the way, if you'd like even more insights into designing your irresistible offer, you can visit our website for more free training and resources:

https://www.brandonehofer.com/free-training

CHAPTER 4
COMMITTING TO THE PATH

Every bit of education that I'm going to give you in this book comes directly from my own life experience, especially the mistakes. In retrospect, all of my errors seem ludicrous, but I didn't have resources like this one readily available to steer me in the right direction.

And one of the biggest mistakes I made early on in coaching other people was not committing to a clear target market right off the bat. Now, eventually I learned how to do this, but when I first started out as a personal trainer, I proudly wore the banner of "I can help anyone with any fitness goal." My heart was in the right place, but my business acumen was seriously lacking.

This is like the life coach who says, "I can help anybody with any limiting belief." It's the business coach who says, "I can help any business owner with any problem." Or it's the digital marketing agency that provides "everything" to help people with their digital presence.

The thought usually goes something like this: I don't want to limit myself, so I'll make my niche as broad as possible so I attract a wider variety of clients. When in actual fact, remaining a generalist is the MOST limiting thing you can do!

Think about it, who makes more? The doctor who is a general practitioner and helps everyone with everything, or the specialist who only performs a few types of ultra-specific brain surgery and is one of only three people on planet Earth who can perform that type of operation. Yup, it's the specialist!

Thing is, if you try to speak to everyone instead of someone, you'll end up reaching no one! And that is more limiting than any niche you could possibly define.

And remember, we're talking about launching your business here. Further down the road, if you want to expand your niche, that's great! But you have to start somewhere, and going too broad from the beginning will not only water down your messaging, but it will dilute your authority.

If you look at my business now, you'll see that I have a transition-niche. Meaning, I help people make one very specific business transition: taking their business online so they can increase their impact and their profit. That's still pretty specific, but when I first started, I wanted it to be laser focused so I could generate momentum as quickly as possible.

As I launched, after branding myself as a life coach for a few months, I quickly realized that I was making the same mistake I did as a new personal trainer, so I made a tactical shift. I designed a 6-month business coaching program specifically for new personal trainers who were working at a big box gym and wanted to transition away from that and start their own personal training company, but had never run their own client-centered business before, so they needed help with everything from branding, to marketing, to sales, and even program design for their clients.

AND, because I wanted to leverage my existing professional network, I decided to start with only fitness professionals who were in my immediate geographic area.

You might think, it doesn't seem like there would be that many fitness professionals in that area who fit that exact description and who are ready right now to make that transition. And you'd be right! But I wasn't trying to get 20 clients right outta the gate. I was just focused on getting my first 2 clients to create momentum. And that's exactly what happened! I enrolled my first 2 clients within 30 days on my new $2,500 offer.

If I had tried to begin with the Online Coach Creator as my first offer, it would have been a disaster! I hadn't yet built up any credibility or authority in that niche, and I would have been seen as just another poser who is trying to "help people go online."

But by creating a super specific niche market and then generating real results for my clients, the program evolved organically. It was my original batch of fitness professional clients who requested I help them create online programs for their clients, and then after that, I got connected with a life coach, a health coach, and a business consultant who reached out to me. They noticed I helped fitness professionals create online businesses, but wanted to know if I could help them too.

And because I was working with a principle based approach, I could absolutely help them.

So now it's time to evaluate your own target market. First of all, do you even have one? I'm serious! I know plenty of enthusiastic people who are legit service providers, but have absolutely no clarity on who they are serving. They are 100% focused on themselves. Just like I was when I first started as a personal trainer! Here's what I mean. When you are coach focused, your primary concern is what you want to do. You might think it will be fun to coach people, but you're more focused on you doing the coaching than you are on creating a specific result for your client. I was there once too! In fact, that's how I got started in the fitness industry, I just thought I would enjoy being a personal trainer and a yoga teacher, so I jumped in.

Being coach focused isn't wrong or bad. It's very often the first step to creating your business because it urges you forward to do something different with your life.

But eventually, after that initial boost into a new venture, you have to shift to becoming client focused. Now you can think from their perspective, and consider what they might need help with.

Let's take that business coach example. Instead of saying "I can help any business owner with any problem," take a look around you at the business owners you already know. Take one out for a coffee and ask them what their most recent challenge has been. How you phrase this question is critical! Don't ask "what's your biggest struggle?" That question never goes anywhere. Instead, give the question a concrete moment in time. By asking what their most recent challenge is, you'll get a story instead of an abstract struggle.

Now they can share with you the details of what's been going on. Do this with a few different business owners. Take notes. And remember, when you translate this into your messaging, you want to speak to someone, not to everyone.

Let's say you end up talking to a few owners of local retail clothing stores. And they tell you a story of how overall they're profitable, but they always seem to run out of cash mid month because of fluctuations in cash flow while payroll and expenses remain steady.

Now you've got something! If you know cash flow is what they cite as their most immediate concern, you can speak to that specific problem.

What's a more effective message for that business owner? "Need to grow your business?" or "Tired of taking out bridge loans every month to cover payroll?" See the difference. One speaks to an actual concrete real life situation. But you never would have come up with that if you had stayed coach-focused, wrapped up in your own world and what you want to do.

And the beautiful irony here is that when you get client-focused, you actually attract new clients who pay you and you get to do what you wanted to do in the first place: Coach people!

Originally, when I was trying to brand myself as a life coach, I was being totally coach-focused. It wasn't until I narrowed down my ideal client that I started actually enrolling people into the Fit Pro Business Launcher program. And then, lo and behold, half of the coaching I ended up engaging in with those clients was life coaching!

Think about it, I got to do the thing I wanted to do, which was life coaching, by selling it as business coaching! Plus, now my program was multifaceted instead of one-dimensional. It was a win-win for everyone involved.

Okay, so you know enough about me by now to know that I'm going to make this insanely practical for you. Because information is great, but it doesn't become transformation until you apply it to your life.

So in the space below, answer the questions provided to help you start identifying your ideal client. And then in the next chapter we'll dig even deeper into how to develop your brand so you actually stand out in a very crowded and noisy marketplace.

IDEAL CLIENT

What characteristics or values does your ideal client have that make them a great fit to work with you?

Briefly describe their current life situation? Use as much detail as possible

What big transition are they about to go through?

What was their most recent life or business challenge?

CHAPTER 5
THE HEART OF YOUR BRAND

One truth that has always resonated with me is "you can't solve the problem if you don't understand the problem."

If we don't make a serious and intense effort to dig in deep and truly understand the pain and desires of our ideal clients, then our service will be mediocre at best, and even potentially harmful.

After you do some initial market research as suggested in Chapter 4, consider whether or not you anticipated what their answers were! More often than not, my private clients who go through this exercise get absolutely floored by their ideal clients' responses. They say things like "I had no idea that they were struggling with XYZ. I'm gonna have to redesign my entire program!"

In a nutshell, we're acknowledging the simplest form of marketing: Discover an existing need and then develop a product or service that fulfills that need. Sounds simple enough right?
But here's the challenge for you: How do you develop a strong brand and forward-facing messaging so you can attract the attention of those you are most qualified to serve?

In other words, it doesn't matter how amazing your service is and how powerful a transformation you can provide if you don't have any clients! The real test of the power of your service will be in how many lives you actually influence and change, not the theoretical effect it could have on someone's life.

So how do we bridge this gap?

These are the top 3 principles when it comes to laying the foundation for powerful messaging that rises above the noise and clutter of the online space and differentiates you as a highly skilled expert.

UNDERSTAND THEIR LEVEL OF AWARENESS

This is simply acknowledging that just because someone has a problem, doesn't mean they know they have that problem. In fact, the symptoms of a problem are usually what someone notices first.

I once read a story from a weight loss coach who reported that one of their clients came to them because he was on an airplane and the seat belt wouldn't reach all the way across his lap, so the flight attendant had to bring out a seat belt extender and hook it up while the other passengers watched. Imagine the embarrassment you'd feel if you were that guy!

So his level of awareness of his problem was "I don't want to feel embarrassed everytime I take a flight." So if you're a weight loss coach, you might be preaching wildly about the long term health risks of obesity and how it affects your cholesterol levels or whatever else. But if the real motivating factor for your ideal client is "I don't want to feel embarrassed in public anymore," then guess what you should focus your marketing messaging on!

On the flip side, if your ideal client is someone who DOES get motivated by long term health-conscious living, then your messaging should absolutely focus on that! See what I'm getting at here? The messaging has got to be custom tailored to the type of person you want to serve.

When I was a personal trainer, I never attracted short-term weight loss clients because my ideal client profile included someone whose value system was aligned with a lifelong approach to movement, strength, and resiliency.

Let's take another example from the world of business coaching. You might be a mindset coach who helps other entrepreneurs overcome their mental blocks around money that are preventing them from enrolling paying clients. So your ideal client might be someone who just keeps doing free sessions for people, but they never make any money, so they have an expensive hobby rather than a business.

That person is probably not even consciously aware of the fact that it's actually a mindset block preventing them from making money in their business. And if they're unaware of that fact, then you can make 100 pieces of video content about how awesome mindset training is, but they won't be paying attention to you!

Instead, if your prospect's level of awareness is, "I can't get a client to pay me," then your marketing messaging might focus on the sales process, or client acquisition, or professional development, or program design, or whatever category you discover that your client THINKS is their issue.

Some call this "Sell them what they want; give them what they need."

Part of being a high level service provider in a client-centered business is to anticipate the needs and desires of your ideal client before they even know that they need you, and then speak to them where they are at, so they notice you and enroll. Then you are in a position to truly help them.

GET CONCRETE AND GRANULAR

Inevitably, as you get clearer on your prospect's level of awareness of their problem, you'll find that you need to get really specific and granular with your messaging.

Here's an example that I've used in the past that got a lot of attention organically on my Facebook profile:

The first time I created an online coaching offer, I thought I was gonna get rich selling a $59 program to thousands of people.

I bought into the myth of "passive" income. Meaning, set it up once and then sit back and watch the Benjamins roll in with no effort on your part.

Know what happened? I worked for 12 months, designing, planning, creating, promoting, advertising, and selling that $59 program. And I made..... zero dollars. Yup, after all things accounted for, I broke even. Except I had just lost a year of my life with nothing to show for it. Eventually, though, I wised up and launched the right way.

If you are putting together a low ticket program or some kind of $49/month membership to launch your online coaching business... spoiler alert... you're headed for disappointment.

Good news is, there's a better way, and I put together a simple video training on exactly how to package your service, position your offer, and get started with your online coaching program so you can build a profitable business and create your lifestyle around it.

There's no opt-in, and no e-mail required, just comment "PLAN" below and I'll send it straight to you.

****

Can you see how I got very specific with the granular details and shared a concrete example of exactly what I did and why it failed?

Because I know that thousands of other online entrepreneurs have made that exact same mistake, I know that this post will speak directly to them.

Then they can opt in with a comment on the post and I follow up with everyone in Messenger with the link for the free training, which is my recorded evergreen masterclass about how to launch their business the right way.

After they watch the training, they have the option to book a call with me to talk about how to move their business forward.

Now imagine if my post had been something like, "Hey coaches, I'm offering free phone calls to help you figure out why your business isn't working right now. Comment below to book a call."

I promise you, there would be crickets on messaging like that because it's vague and doesn't show the reader that I know what they're going through.

When you share concrete experience, your prospect can relate based on their own experience as well.

TELL STORIES OF PEOPLE LIKE THEM

Finally, your messaging should focus on sharing stories of people just like your ideal client, so they can move past the question everyone is asking: "Will it work *for me?*"

Back when I was focused on helping personal trainers leave their gym and launch their own fitness coaching businesses, I would share stories like Jason's:

"Can you believe that after 4 years of working at the gym, next month your boy is going to be out? I transitioned most of my clients to an online program and have already enrolled over $7,500 in new clients for my new signature program. I couldn't have done this without the Online Coach Creator, and I'm so excited to start a new life for myself running my own business! You've got to do the strategy session with Brandon. That was the biggest starting point for me when he helped me get massive clarity on what I really wanted."

But if I wanted to get the attention of someone who paid for another coach in the past and had a negative experience, I would share Keira's story:

"I need you all to know how much Brandon's program changed things for me, because I literally was about to throw in the towel when he reached out to me. I wasted over $20,000 on other coaches and got nowhere. But within the first 30 days of Online Coach Creator I enrolled my first two high-end clients at over $1,000/month."

And so when you are putting together your marketing messaging, you can anticipate what your prospect's objections will be and then find stories of past clients who had the same objection and discovered that working with you truly works!

Now, if you are brand new as a service provider, you might have to first generate some testimonials with a beta-launch or even an adjusted rate. That's okay!

Some gurus will tell you to charge full price right outta the gate, but if you've never coached someone before, that may not be appropriate. Instead, focus on serving a few clients, getting awesome results for them, and then collecting some testimonials.

A word of caution though, if this is all you do without eventually moving forward and charging your full rate, then you might need to hire that mindset coach I mentioned above.

By compiling your client testimonials and having these available in case studies or testimonial banks, you show your future clients that people like them have gotten the same results that they are after.

And of course this assumes that you know what your clients are after in terms of outcomes from working with you.

If you think they want lower cholesterol and they actually want to be able to use a single seat belt, then it's time to go back to the drawing board and use the exercise below to get clarity on those you intend to serve.

GETTING CLARITY

1. What is your client's biggest frustration right now?

2. What is your client's greatest desire?

3. What is the thing they need to solve most urgently?

4. What just happened in their life that prompted them to look for support?

5. What is the thing they *think* is their problem?

6. What is their actual problem?

CHAPTER 6
CRAFTING YOUR IRRESISTIBLE OFFERS

The only thing standing between you and the income of your dreams is your ability to clearly articulate to your ideal client exactly how you can help them change their life.

Your income will rise in direct proportion to your ability to clearly define your offer and then clearly explain that process to your prospect so they feel confident in their choice to work with you.

For whatever reason, creating a structured process for clients is one of the biggest obstacles for new service providers. It's easy enough to dream up end results or outcomes, but rarely does the new entrepreneur take the time to design a predictable process around their service.

But this is the only way to rise above the session by session or hour by hour mindset. This is also the only way to articulately guarantee the results that you produce. Once you have a predictable process in place, the only variable is whether or not your clients actually show up and do their part.

My own experience with this principle was when I was making the transition to online coaching. I wanted to serve people with life coaching at first, but then got clear on my ideal client, and so my coaching niche evolved a bit.

And for awhile, I was charging people session by session for coaching. Even when I made the leap to a monthly retainer model, I was still only charging $297/month for 1:1 coaching. It wasn't until I packaged everything up into one single premium offer that I was able to charge $2,500 for a fully comprehensive program that included 1:1 sessions, group coaching, digital training, assets and templates, tech coaching, and a few other resources to help my clients reach their intended outcomes.

Eventually, that $2,500 program became a $12,000 program because I kept refining it and making it better and better with each passing month. In fact, I'm continuing to make it better to this day, so it will just keep evolving.

The process I want to walk you through in this chapter is not just how to create one single premium program, but to also introduce a few other tiers of service so that you have a full suite of offers.

I also go through this process in that video I mentioned in the Phase 2 introduction. So here's that link again for your reference:

https://www.brandonehofer.com/free-training

I recommend watching that video now, and then coming back to this chapter to make even more progress on your business.

THE PREMIUM OFFER

This is the best place to begin. If you are a coach or consultant, this is your 1:1 VIP Coaching experience. If you are a service provider with a done-for-you service, this is your top tier package with all the bells and whistles. This is where you ask yourself "what would it take for me to do my BEST work with a perfect client. And if they also showed up fully invested in the process, what will the outcomes be?"

Can you feel the difference between that premise and "how low can I get my prices so someone will hire me?"

The first one comes from a place of abundance and genuine service. It is client-focused. On the flip side, wondering how you can get someone to hire you is very coach-focused. At that level, which is very low frequency, you are concerned only with yourself.

Thing is, there will always be someone who wants your absolute highest quality support and service, and they are willing to pay a premium rate to get that level of support.

Now, it's extremely popular on the interwebs these days to call this approach "high-ticket" and to then claim that this is the only way to do it, and that you should never have a low ticket or entry level offer because it somehow devalues your premium experience.

Nothing could be further from the truth.

The existence of other service offerings and lower price points only reinforces how amazing your premium service is, because not everyone will be able to access it, and that's okay. There are folks for whom price is a legitimate condition and not just an objection, and if you still want to serve those folks, you'll need a different type of program for them.

But how do you design your predictable process?

First, ask yourself what are the primary obstacles that someone has to overcome in order to reach their goal. And then, what are the milestones they achieve along the way that help them overcome those obstacles and create a new reality for themselves.

In case you haven't noticed yet, this entire book is my predictable process. Each chapter outlines one of the predictable barriers you must overcome to reach the outcome of having a profitable and sustainable online client-centered business.

After working with hundreds of entrepreneurs and guiding them through this process, I already know what obstacles you are going to encounter and I can give you the blueprint to get through all of them.

Your fieldwork exercise for this chapter will be to codify your proprietary process so that you know exactly where your clients are headed. This gives you clarity as the coach, but it also gives your clients the reassurance that you know where they're headed so they can feel confident along the way.

Why is that so vital? Because the number one reason entrepreneurs either fail or just quit at this mission is because they begin to doubt that what they are doing is the right path. So they hesitate, and the business dies a slow painful death.

Once you've laid out your premium offer, it's time to start enrolling people to validate that offer before you dive into creating your next two tiers of service. This is a crucial step and not to be skipped! I've seen too many entrepreneurs who create what they think are incredible offers and then after 6 months of frustration realize that the offer isn't selling and have to scrap the entire thing and start from scratch.

Assuming that your prospecting and enrollment process is dialed in, which we'll cover in Phase 3 of this book, you should be enrolling new clients within 30 days to validate your offer, which simply means confirming that it's a viable product and that people are willing to pay money for it.

But before you scrap your program and start again, just remember, 30 days to validate assumes that you are doing the real work of attracting leads and then making numerous attempts at enrolling them. I'm not saying that if 10 people don't want your offer, then it's time to go back to the drawing board. I'm saying that you have to get your sales skills honed in first, and *then* you can determine whether or not it's the offer that isn't a good fit, the audience that isn't a good fit, or if you just need to work on objection handling.

We'll cover the basics of Value-Driven Enrollment in Chapter 8, but if you'd like to dig in deep and learn how to effortlessly enroll prospects without resistance, then you'll want to preview The Sales Mastery Accelerator Program, which you can learn more about by visiting this link:

https://www.brandonehofer.com/mastery

THE LEVERAGED OFFER

Next, after you've got your Premium Offer dialed in, it's time to create a Leveraged Offer. As you start to fill your schedule with 1:1 clients or done-for-you services, you'll need to create something that keeps revenue flowing through the door, but that also leverages your time.

For a coach, this could be a group coaching format, or even a leveraged 1:1 model with fewer or shorter sessions with you, but more guided fieldwork assignments between sessions so your client continues to make progress.

The critical evaluation criteria for this offer is asking yourself whether the leveraged offer creates more time for you as the service provider **and** also creates a better or more accelerated result for your client. If you can't answer yes to both then it's back to the drawing board.

In my own business, I've created a group coaching program that is just $297/month at the time of this writing. It allows anyone to participate in coaching directly with me, without the price tag that my VIP clients pay. Plus, I can serve hundreds of clients at any given time inside a group coaching program.

So it allows me to serve more people in less time while simultaneously providing the same quality of experience for my clients. It's a win-win.

You'll get other gurus out there who say you *must* do group coaching, and that group coaching is the only way to run a business and you have to get rid of 1:1 all together.

This is flat out wrong. Unless you absolutely hate coaching people or serving them 1:1, then you should definitely keep that as an option for your clients, but just make sure you charge an appropriate fee, because there's only so much of you to go around and there are many other activities involved with running a coaching business, beyond just the sessions or done-for-you service hours.

Once you have your Leveraged Offer up and running, you can begin to create your entry-level program.

THE AUTOMATED PROGRAM

Now, to be clear, this one is called "automated" because it involves less or your time, but it isn't 100% automated. You still have to pay attention to it and refine it over time, it's just that the delivery of the experience takes only tiny fractions of your time compared to the other two tiers of service.

And when it comes to these entry level offers, there's really not one "right" answer. I've seen service providers and coaches successful with everything from $7/month membership programs to $497 one-time purchases. It just depends on the nature of the offer.

But here's the thing - behind all the peripheral issues of pricing and what not, the main idea here is that this offer is primarily for lead generation and nurture. The book you are holding in your hands is one of my "automated" offers. My goal is to break even on ad spend and then welcome you into my eco-system of awesome training resources, education, and coaching.

Many of you will read the book and I'll never hear from you again. That's fine, as long as you take this information to heart and go apply it so you can dominate the online space. Others will read the book and maybe join my Facebook group, and somewhere down the road you might decide that my Leveraged Program or my Premium Program is a good fit for you. That's cool too!

The point is, your automated offer, in whatever form it takes, has to genuinely help someone take the first few steps in their journey.

Let's say you are a fitness coach. You might want to launch a $7/month offer filled with pre-recorded workouts, exercise tutorials, and meal plan templates. You can upload all these resources to a digital delivery platform such as Kajabi and then the delivery of that program will be mostly automated. Then you could create a Facebook group for everyone who joins that $7/month membership, and do a live coaching or QnA session once per week. Then each of those live coaching sessions can be uploaded to the digital training portal so the value of the product grows over time and is never stagnant.

Or let's say you are an investment coach. You might not want to do group coaching if you are dealing with people's private or sensitive information. But you could create a simple educational workshop around the principles or investment strategies you use. You could host the workshop live each month and charge people a one-time fee of $97.

In this way, your tribe gets rock solid wisdom for how to think about investment options, and then you can offer them another workshop or invite them to a recurring membership.

Always just keep in mind, what does your ideal client need to take that first step. For me, I know that a big obstacle for most people leaping into the online space is the uncertainty of not knowing what to do to establish themselves online. So I wrote this book with that in mind, so that the book can alleviate this uncertainty and make you see the path forward.

In other words, I want to help you believe deep down, without a doubt, that you *can* indeed make this online business work.

YOUR PROGRAM PROCESS

But let's not get too far ahead of ourselves here. The priority task for you today is to create a rough skeleton of your Premium Program so you can start to gain clarity on what you will be providing. This is designing the money maker!

What is the problem you solve or the transition you help someone through? Think in terms of current state vs. desired state.

Write down the main obstacles you know with certainty that your ideal client will encounter as they move from current state to desired state.

Now write down the primary milestones or achievements they accomplish along the way.

BONUS - Now give each phase a creative name to help with differentiating your program

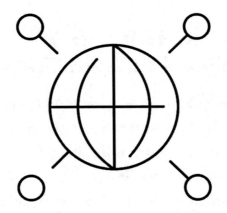

PHASE 3
ONLINE GROWTH

If you've actually done the work up until this point, you are ready to start making money online. You now have a transformational offer to bring to the world. So where do you find people who want and need your service?

They are literally everywhere! In this Phase, we'll explore how to find those you are most qualified to serve without getting overwhelmed and lost in the vast expanse of the internet.

After working through this section you'll have a laser focused plan of action rather than a vague sense of needing a client. You'll know precisely where to look so you are talking to the right people so you can begin enrolling right away.

CHAPTER 7
BUILDING YOUR TRIBE

When it comes to building a targeted audience, there are a few guiding principles that determine your best course of action. The first one is simply this: Attention is the Asset. In other words, getting someone's attention is the best way to bring them into your tribe. Sounds simple enough, right? Get more eyeballs on you and your digital presence and you will win.

In the olden days of the internet, e-mail was the front-runner in attention grabbing power. Now, I'm not one of these "e-mail is dead" kinda coaches. E-mail certainly has its place in the Spider-Web Marketing Strategy, which is what we'll explore in this Phase, but it is no longer the front-runner simply for the mere fact that there are more eyeballs spending more time on social media platforms than ever before.

And these days, there are hundreds upon hundreds of different social media platforms. And yes, if you are a Pinterest expert, by all means use Pinterest. But as of this writing, the Big 4 are still the best place to establish your online presence and then leverage to build your business.

Those Big 4 are Facebook, YouTube, LinkedIn, and Instagram. This obviously could fluctuate wildly over the next few years or decades, but given the fact that they have survived the initial testing ground of longevity, it is likely that they will all be around for decades to come.

We could easily get lost on rabbit trail after rabbit trail talking about all of these, so for the sake of keeping this chapter high impact and actionable, I'm going to discuss launching with your focus on Facebook. That's how I got my start in this business, and that's the path I recommend to all my clients because Facebook already has so many communities and pre-existing groups established, which makes it very easy to begin connecting with hundreds and then thousands of your ideal clients.

THE FACEBOOK TRIFECTA

The Facebook echo chamber can either be your final undoing or it can create new opportunities in your life. The echo chamber means that Facebook prioritizes keeping you on the platform for longer and longer because they make money by selling advertising. So it stands to reason that if they have more eyeballs on more of their stuff all the time, then the value of their platform to advertisers goes up and up.

And one of the ways Facebook accomplishes this is to create a type of echo chamber, so they actually want to feed you more and more of the stuff you already like and believe in. If they think you're interested in a post, they will feed you that post again and again to keep you engaged.

Why does this matter for you as a business owner? Because the more you can get your face and ideas in front of the eyeballs of your ideal client, the more they will start to experience you as part of their echo chamber. And when you are the coach who is top of mind for them, you immediately become a voice of authority for that topic.

One of the ways to begin building this "eco-system" on Facebook is to leverage the trifecta of your Personal Profile, a Facebook Business Page, and a Facebook Group. These are 3 separate entities on Facebook, and you will need all of them to be successful.

While we're on this topic, if you want a more in-depth training on how to best utilize a Facebook Business Page, and what to do *before* you launch any paid ads, check out the link below:

https://www.brandonehofer.com/facebook

With your Personal Profile, you'll build an audience through engagement and friend requests. With your Facebook Group, you'll build community through invitation and interaction. And with your Facebook Business Page, you'll create authority and expansion with paid ads and retargeting.

A lot of people who I work with are initially hesitant to use their Personal Profile to connect with potential clients and meet new people. They are also hesitant to start leveraging call-to-action posts that invite people to comment on their stuff in exchange for resources and lead magnets.

The thought process is usually some version of this: "Well, I don't want to do that because what if Timmy from high school thinks what I'm doing is dumb and he's not interested." Or "I think a few of my relatives that I talk to once every 4 years might get offended that I'm a coach for xyz now, because they don't understand what I'm doing."

And on and on and on. At the heart of these and every other version of this excuse is an underlying problem that we have to sort through from day 1, because it doesn't matter if you are launching an online business with social media or if you are trying to become a world-class speaker and author. There is an insidious force that will crush every opportunity you have to succeed in this realm unless you destroy it today.

That force is self-imposed and it is when you concern yourself with anyone else's judgement of you. The brilliant thinker Abraham Maslow called it being independent of the good opinion of others. In other words, you will actually stop considering what Timmy from high school thinks of what you're doing... because *you* want to do it. You will stop giving power to those around you, even sometimes family members you care about, by letting them dictate what your mission should be.

And that's what at the heart of this: Your mission. If you are truly connected to what you are doing and you believe that you have an incredible gift to give to the world through your service-based business, then it won't bother you even if someone else on your Personal Profile from 8 years ago might think your business isn't a good idea.

And to be perfectly straightforward here, if someone is connected with you on social media, and they don't support what you're doing, you have the power to click "unfollow" or even "unfriend." You don't have to cut them out of your life completely (except in some cases... that's also a whole other book), but you can choose which platforms they can interact with you on.

Here's one that used to hold me back. "I've made the leap from personal trainer to successful online coach, and I want to promote how awesome that is... but what if one of my personal trainer friends sees my stuff and gets offended because they think I'm putting down what they're doing." For a long time, I allowed that thought to hold me back from being bold with my messaging online. I want people to know that the session by session business model is a dead end, even if you're great at it!

And eventually I just had to take responsibility for my mission, and if someone chooses to be offended by my message, then they're not an ideal client for me anyway.

So if you've ever felt hesitant to be bold with your messaging online, and to proudly proclaim your mission, then now is the time to choose a new belief and push forward, especially if you've been thinking about making this online business a reality and you've been holding back.

And slowly over time, you will refine your Personal Profile to be thousands and thousands of your ideal clients and the people who aren't interested in you will just fade away. And that's totally fine, and totally awesome!

THE COCKTAIL PARTY

So where do you find these folks who fit your ideal client profile? Well, in the land of Facebook, there are already thousands of pre-existing communities where your ideal clients are hanging out.

When I first got started in online coaching, my program was specifically designed for fitness professionals who needed help with business building.

So I found a group full of 20,000 other fitness professionals. And it was easy to find because the name of the group was very clear about who the group is for.

So I joined that group and started connecting with people. Now, let me be clear here, what you should *not* do is jump in a group and start posting links and promoting yourself. That'll get you kicked out faster than you joined.

Instead, think of a Facebook group as one big cocktail party. You hang out, mingle, make comments, ask questions, and ultimately you want to send that friend request and see if they want to connect in Messenger for a one-on-one chat.

And here's the best part. As you connect with more and more of your ideal clients, Facebook will start to realize who you are most interested in and then suggest similar types of people.

At one point, when I was focused just on fitness professionals, in the "People You May Know" section, Facebook suggested nothing but fitness professionals with a few other people scattered in.

That's what I mean by the power of the echo chamber, which is just another reason to get really specific with your niche, because then Facebook's algorithm is incentivized to help you find more of the people you are looking for!

After you've created a strong audience on your Personal Profile, it's time to create what's known as a "Call-to-Action" post to attract more of those ideal clients to consume more of your content on the path to knowing you, liking you, and trusting you more and more.

The idea is to produce a valuable piece of content, what's called a Lead Magnet, and then offer it to your audience. This lead magnet should help someone take the first step in your transformational process or it should give them insight into the process that you coach them through and how your process can help them with their problem or life transition.

We won't get too much into the details of copywriting in this book, but if you'd like to see a solid call-to-action post generate 43 new leads with one post, just go to the link below:

https://www.brandonehofer.com/43-new-leads

In the next chapter, we'll talk about the enrollment process, which is how you take someone from interested prospect to raving-fan client, but for now, just consider the power of an organic call to action post like this one that generates 43 new leads.

You could pay Google or Facebook a bunch of money in ad spend to create new leads, and you won't even be sure if they are good leads or not. Or, you can spend $0 and just a few hours a week building your audience organically and then with a single post start one-to-one conversations with each of them and use those opportunities to book enrollment calls.

This is how I made my first $50,000 online before I even started using paid ads to expand my reach. And I know other coaches who use organic reach exclusively and have made hundreds of thousands online without paid traffic. The point is, these strategies work. And as a bonus, when you test out your messaging organically, you can evaluate which messaging resonates most powerfully with your audience *before* you start to put money behind it. Paid traffic will only accelerate and amplify what's already happening organically, so let's make sure you have it dialed in before you start pumping a bunch of your hard earned dollars into ads.

I know there are a lot of programs out there who tell you that you can create one webinar and then just "turn on the faucet" of Facebook ads, and for every $1 you put in, you'll magically get $5 back. But it doesn't work like that. Even the big dogs with millions of dollars in ad spend still leverage organic traffic as the foundation of what they do.

So if you'll commit to building a strong organic audience with quality ideal clients, and if you'll commit to showing up every day to do the work to make that happen, you will be wildly successful in this business and you'll be able to fully live out your mission while building the life you deserve.

CHAPTER 8
VALUE DRIVEN ENROLLMENT

Sales. Typically there are two categories of business owners when it comes to sales. The first one loves the process! It's exhilarating to feel the surge of adrenaline and serotonin that floods your brain as you close the deal and someone swipes their card for thousands of dollars in exchange for a promised return of a brighter future.

And then there's the second, who loves serving people and coaching them and letting someone else leverage their wisdom and experience, but for some reason that initial exchange of money inspires all kinds of feelings of nervousness, anxiety, fear, and sometimes even a state of paralysis!

The purpose of this chapter is not to somehow convince you that you "should" learn to love sales. Because after all, "should-ing" all over yourself never leads to personal or professional growth.

Instead, I'm going to show you why the enrollment process is no different than the coaching process itself. And the coaching process is nothing more than helping to guide someone through their decision making process, to overcome ambivalence, and to make a firm commitment to move their life or business forward.

And even if you don't call yourself a "coach" as your professional title, that's okay. Even if you run a digital marketing agency or provide ad management services, you can still learn and develop the skill of coaching as a way to guide your clients through their own decision making process and into a mutually beneficial relationship with you.

I've been "selling" things for 20 years now, and I've inspired people to buy everything from a $17 knife to a six-figure home remodel project. And along the way, I've picked up a few guiding principles that have allowed me to rise above the standard method of teaching sales tactics and to instead educate people on principles of influence.

But this wisdom didn't truly click for me until after I had been selling one particular type of service for a few years - Personal Training.

The enrollment model I use today, and that you'll learn in this chapter, was originally inspired by a model of fitness coaching enrollment. And when I broke it down to extract the principles behind the words I was using, I realized that the model works for anyone who is selling a service through which the buyer is seeking a brighter future through an engagement with the service provider.

And that's what at the heart of all of this. Can you inspire someone to choose *first* to make a new commitment to themselves and *then* to agree to work specifically with you to help them accomplish that.

The fanciest sales presentations won't make even the slightest difference in someone's life if they haven't first made the decision to do the thing that you are qualified to help them with.

Make sense? Secure the commitment to act first, then you can make the case for why your program or service is the best path to get them to that new commitment.

Let's dig in.

THE SESSION BY SESSION STRUGGLE

Like many other coaches, I made the evolution to rise above the session by session business model by necessity. In my early days as a personal trainer, I was having a hard time getting someone to buy even a single session for $40. I fell into the trap of believing that I had to keep lowering my prices to get someone to buy something from me.

It's the old "race to the bottom," and it never works.

But eventually I came face to face with a harsh reality. Coaches coach. And if I don't have any clients, then I might say I'm a personal trainer, but in actual fact, I'm not. I'm just a guy without an income!

So after struggling for awhile, I finally decided that I'm gonna either make this thing work in the next 3 months, or I have to go get a jobby-job just to pay the bills. That was when it clicked. I knew that I had to either make sales and train people or just walk away.

The very next day, I had a meeting with someone who would be my first $720 personal training package sale. Looking back now $720 seems so absurdly low for the value of the service I was providing, but at the time, I was amped up to make that sale and go to work!

So what changed? How did I make that first sale and then go on to sell packages way beyond a mere $720?

I finally learned to just relax and instead of trying to impress my client with my vast knowledge of physical training, I just listened. I learned what her motivations were for looking for a trainer in the first place. I asked her questions to figure out if she was ready to make this commitment now. And only *after* she said yes to herself did we talk about the actual service and the pricing.

From there I started developing an actual structure around my enrollment process, and like clockwork my enrollment percentage began to climb steadily over the course of the next few years.

The reason a process used in fitness coaching translates so well to other types of coaching and service-based business is because the premise is exactly the same. I'm guiding someone through a process, and they are paying me up front for my time, expertise, and predictable processes.

Think about it, when someone buys a fitness coaching program, they are usually looking to transform their body in some way in order to enhance some other area of their life. Perhaps lose weight to reverse the effects of type-II diabetes, or renew their joint range of motion to eliminate pain so they can play with their grandkids, or develop their physical strength as a way to feel strong and capable in other areas of life, or even just to look better to attract a mate.

But at the core of the purchase is the hope that this different future is possible! And if you're selling *any* service or coaching program, that's at the heart of your value proposition as well. Someone is willing to pay you money because they are motivated to discover a new future and then create that new future with you.

At one point in my career, as I was transitioning into the online coaching space, I had an opportunity to sell coaching programs for another coach. I would take the inbound sales calls and then enroll them into an $8,000 coaching program.

Typically, when someone has a program they want to sell in this manner, they will position their sales team as a "Strategy Coach" or something similar, which is what gets the prospect to book the call, because they think they are getting coaching. And notoriously, the typical sales rep massively under-delivers on that promise because they haven't actually developed a true coaching skill, so the prospect feels lied to and walks away.

So when I got the opportunity to enroll people in this position, I took my role as coach very seriously! I ended up using my skill as a coach to guide people through the decision making process and enroll them into the program. During that season, it wasn't uncommon for people to ask if I would be their coach for the full program after they enroll!

Through that experience I learned that if I could use this coaching skillset to enroll people into someone else's coaching program, then I could certainly use it to enroll people into my own coaching program, and that's exactly what I did!

So rather than give you a rigid script to follow, I want to highlight a few key foundations for how you approach your enrollment process.

SALES MASTERY

The first foundation is that sales tactics are the weakest form of sales training. They are one-dimensional and rely on a belief that your prospect is *not* an intelligent and capable person. Instead, it assumes they are easily manipulated and if you speak the "magic words" in the right order, then they will definitely buy from you.

In this family of training materials are things like "101 super duper closes" and the like. But random one-liners applied out of context will not inspire your prospect to make a life changing decision. It might inspire them to buy a VitaMix at Costco, but not to invest $12,000 in a 6 month coaching program that will change the trajectory of their entire life.

This is not to say that there aren't specific skills involved and certain words or phrases that can be more influential than others. Instead, it's simply acknowledging that everything happens in context. And your pursuit as the coach should be to first establish a strong connection of trust, because ultimately you will be acting as their guide and if they don't trust you, they won't allow themselves to be coached by, even if it's free.

The next foundation is acknowledging the overlap between the sales process and the coaching process. I know, I know, I already told you this, but now it's time to integrate it into your life. If you won't commit to the process of becoming fully present and understand the psychology behind a person's motivation to change, then you'll forever be stuck relying on tactics, and the delivery of your program will also suffer.

To this end, I highly recommend you pick up the book Motivational Interviewing, 3rd Edition by William R. Miller and Stephen Rollnick. It's not a sales book at all, but it's the best book I've ever read on the process of helping someone come to a firm decision to move their life forward one way or the other.

It will even teach you about the process of evoking the emotion within, which is at the heart of the coaching process.

Fact is, deciding ***whether*** to change is the prerequisite for planning ***how*** to change. And if the ***how*** is a program with you as their guide, then your prospect must first own their decision of ***whether*** to change or not. It's no coincidence that the people who don't enroll in your program are still stuck in the exact same life situation two years later when you check in with them. They will tell you it's the price, but it's not. It's their unwillingness to simply choose. And if the seed of desire to change is there, we would do our future clients a disservice by not helping to cultivate that seed so that it can grow and their dream can be realized.

The third foundation is that carefully selected Powerful Questions invite a new decision. I use a clever little acronym for sales structure called FITPROS where each letter stands for a necessary part of the coaching and evoking process for the sales call. And no, it's not just for fitness professionals, I just developed it in that context and decided I still like how clever it is, so I kept the acronym, and it's still just as applicable.

The "P" in FITPROS stands for Powerful Questions, which is where you as the service provider anticipate what challenges or obstacles your prospect is facing and then you ask them insightful questions to help them see the path forward.

Easy, right?

Not quite. Each one of your questions must be carefully selected based on the needs and desires of your prospect and their level of awareness of their problem.

In my context, most coaches think their problem is marketing, when their first problem is really that they don't have a clearly defined offer. 100 more eyeballs won't do you any good if you don't know what you're selling!

So if I ask someone what inspired them to reach out to chat with me and they say something like, "I need more leads," I might then ask a question like "who is an ideal client for you?" and "what is your signature program" and "describe your predictable program process to me."

98% of the time, they have no idea! So then we get to pull it back a bit to the basics and I can help them see that although there is a time for marketing, it's not the best next step for them today.

I once spent 6 weeks back and forth with someone in Facebook Messenger coaching him on developing his core signature offer *before* we even spoke on the phone. He enrolled, and a few weeks after that we finally put the finishing touches on his offer.

The fourth foundation is that you can actually add legitimate value to the enrollment process. And yes, it's true that there are many coaches out there who use this type of language, but don't live up to it. They claim that they are adding "massive value," but the entire enrollment conversation is just a giant sales pitch. I've been on the receiving end of these conversations, and it just felt gross.

I've also been on the receiving end of enrollment conversations that were conducted masterfully and actually did give me new insight and provided a clear strategy to move forward.

If you conduct yourself masterfully as a coach during the enrollment call, there are many ways to add value, but the ones that stand out the most are Clarity, Strategy, and Invitation.

Clarity is perhaps the most significant, and also the most challenging to execute properly. But if you leverage well-crafted powerful questions, you can help someone make realizations and breakthroughs that they've never experienced before. You'll give them the real emotional experience of working with you, which makes collecting payment that much easier when the time comes.

Strategy means helping someone see the path forward. I can spend an hour on the phone with someone and help them understand, for example, that their most immediate problem isn't finding new leads but rather developing a strong signature program that they can sell. (More on that in Phase 5). By clarifying what they actually want to accomplish with their business (remember, life by design first), we'll be able to carve out what practical steps they need to make that happen.

Which leads into the third item of value - Invitation. This is the simplest form of enrollment, because if you give someone a clear cut path of action, it's super easy and non-invasive to simply ask "would you like help putting that into action?" Meaning, you can give someone the roadmap, but then it's also incredibly valuable to offer your expert guidance as they implement that roadmap.

And then the fifth foundation in the enrollment process is acknowledging that all objections are just limiting beliefs in disguise. And the primary limiting belief archetype is "I lack the necessary resource to move forward." I mean, think about it, any time you give an objection or excuse in your life, even if the exchange of money is not involved, it's always because you mistakenly think that you lack the time, money, skill, discipline, knowledge, relationships, etc, to move forward with that decision.

I don't have the money for a personal trainer; I don't know how to start a new business; I don't have the right connections to make good investments; I'm not a disciplined person, so I can't start a savings account; I don't have an advanced degree, so I can't get ahead in life.

See what I mean? It's always the belief that you lack one or more necessary resources.

Here's the truth: once you make a firm commitment to a decision, you'll figure out a way to find, create, or borrow whatever resources you need.

So in the context of you as the coach in the enrollment conversation, you have to first acknowledge that all of ***your*** excuses are just limiting beliefs in disguise, so that you can then coach someone else on overcoming their limiting beliefs and make the choice to work with you.

Now, obviously I'm making the assumption that the prospect you're talking to is actually a good fit for your program and also feels connected to you and your process. If you are enrolling people that you cannot help, that's a different problem, and you won't make it far as a service provider.

So your responsibility as coach is to guide the person first to the commitment itself, then to helping them mentally work through the limiting beliefs that are holding them back so they can begin the process of transformation with you.

For details on a much more in depth training and experience of the Value-Driven Enrollment model go to the following link:

https://www.brandonehofer.com/mastery

You'll see an invitation to enroll in a powerful 30-day sales mastery process.

CHAPTER 9
RISING ABOVE THE NOISE

Client fulfillment systems are not the sexiest topic, but they are absolutely necessary and they are actually the lifeblood to the longevity of any client-centered business.

Most online service providers emphasize front-end sales and marketing efforts, which are necessary to get in front of more prospects. But if you don't equally emphasize the client experience through your program, you'll end up losing millions of dollars long term.

Think of it this way, the more money I must spend on acquiring a client, the more I have to artificially inflate my pricing to make up for the increased marketing and advertising costs.

But if I serve all my clients at a high level, and I stand out in an industry that is full of fluff and posers, then I multiply the likelihood that someone will continue to work with me long term, which allows you to keep your marketing costs down so you can focus on investing a portion of your profits into a better client experience, which in turn creates even more long term profit.
Can you see why this emphasis is so critical to your business long term?

The question then is how do you rise above the noise? How do you stand out in a saturated market place where the barrier to entry is low, but so few stick around long term?

I faced this dilemma early on as a fitness professional. Thing is, anyone can go get "certified" by taking a 30-Day course, and now they are somehow qualified to create fitness programs for the masses. But my mission was never to just get a certification and make a quick buck. I wanted to hone my craft and get better and better as I went.

As a result I invested thousands and thousands of dollars into continuing education and seminars and workshops so I could rise above the average personal trainer. And as I got better and better, I started attracting more and more the type of client I truly wanted to work with long term, and that led to my clients getting awesome results and having a blast doing it!

And that in turn led to what we call "social proof." In other words, now prospective clients, who are unconsciously asking "will this work for me?" can look at someone similar to them who is already working with me and get the inside scoop of what it's like to be a client of mine.

And what did my clients emphasize? The lifelong approach of course! Because that was part of our shared value system, which then helped attract other people who were also looking for that particular approach to fitness.

Here's what this means for you - the only way to truly rise above the noise and get out of the never ending Entrepreneur's Hamster Wheel of market-sell-market-sell is to design your program to be high impact in the short term, but truly transformational in the long term.

In order to create a system of predictable client creation that inevitably leads to client retention, you'll have to focus on the 4 areas of client longevity - Attraction, Connection, Retention, and Perfection.

ATTRACTION

This is where most marketing programs have you focus on 100% of your time and attention. You know the type - "Buy our program and we'll show you how to get leads on autopilot."
Thing is, leads aren't necessarily valuable to you. Not unless they are the right kind of leads that fit with what you're offering. And even if you get thousands upon thousands of new leads from a paid cold traffic campaign, and even if a decent percentage of them are truly a good fit, you still have to expend a massive amount of time, money, and energy to enroll them and then go back out and acquire new leads.

This Attraction-Only mentality creates an environment where you'll always be spending a vast majority of your time looking for new clients, which inevitably creates less time for client service and real outcomes for those you serve.

To actively combat this tendency towards Attraction-Only marketing, we've got to add another layer.

CONNECTION

This will sound painfully obvious to anyone who already intuitively wants to connect with their tribe on a real human level, but true connection often gets lost in the mix. If my only product is an automated course that creates zero interaction with my client base, then I'll never be able to truly connect with them.

Instead, by enrolling someone into a program with you as their coach or service provider, and then by connecting with them on a personal level, you not only eliminate buyer's remorse and unnecessary chargebacks, you also create a stronger bond that will later create additional opportunities to serve this client and make a profit doing so.

If it costs me $500 to acquire a new client, then I don't want to keep spending that $500 again and again. I'd much rather put a little more effort into serving my client on a very personal level and then re-enrolling them into ongoing programs or ancillary programs that continue to benefit them

Back when I was a personal trainer at the local big box gym, after a few years, most of my clients were long term connections that continued to see me year after year on a twice a week or three times a week frequency.

And I was quite good at selling personal training services, so it's not like I couldn't have gone out and found more clients whenever I wanted to. It was just so exhausting to spend that much time building a clientele.

It was so much more seamless and effortless to just serve my existing clients in the best way possible, and to overdeliver, so that they just kept coming back again and again.

And the same is true of an online coaching business. If you spend a bunch of time and effort gathering new clients organically through the methods we discussed in chapter 7, then doesn't it make sense to keep those folks in your eco-system for as long as possible rather than constantly starting from scratch?

I actually made this mistake early on in my online coaching business.

When I first launched, I had one premium offer for one specific client to solve one specific problem. Nothing wrong with that. In fact, I recommend that's how to start. But I hesitated to create the other two tiers of service for my 3-tier model (more on that in Phase

5). As a result, as soon as my clients were done with the 6 month program, I had nothing else to enroll them in.

Eventually I wised up and created multiple 30-Day Accelerator Programs as well as a month to month continuity program for those who wanted and needed additional help.

With these new offers, I could maintain connection long term with my clients, which naturally led to higher retention.

RETENTION

I hope you can see how all 4 of these principles of client longevity are really just one long continuum of stellar service. If you attract the right people, connect with them in a meaningful way as you serve them, then client retention will be the natural outcome.

But client retention is more than just people paying you money consistently over time. The real foundation of client retention is the willingness on the part of the coach to move dynamically through life with their clients. This takes place when the coach can move beyond the structure of the coaching program and address the deeper needs of the client, specifically around emotional and spiritual growth, as well as the inner desire to leave a lasting legacy.

You can serve a client well for a few months and help them to do a thing better. For example, I can help you get better at marketing and sales so you make more money in your business. That's a good outcome. But if you stick with me long term, we're gonna go much deeper than that. We've got to dig into the legacy you are leaving with your entire life, and then create long term visionary plans based on those desires.

I'm talking about the pursuits that take much more than 6 months to accomplish, the things that take years, even decades to establish.

Transactional sales will make you a little money in the short term, but true client retention based on the pursuit of legacy, will make you wealthy and establish your authority as a high impact coach in your space.

PERFECTION

Now, when I say perfection, I don't mean "without error," but rather that feeling you get when everything just works together as a cohesive whole. Some call this "flow state," or "synchronicity," but whatever you call it, you'll know it when it happens.

You get a deep sense of fulfillment and satisfaction when you are making money, changing lives, living within your superpower and true identity, and you've eliminated the stress of the grind because you're focused on long term outcomes rather than short term profits.

Once you turn your attention to pursuing this type of business, you'll find that your system of client acquisition begins to take on a life of its own and you will truly rise above the noise in a crowded industry. Not because you are a better marketer, but because you are a better coach.

PHASE 4
THE RIGHT TOOLS FOR THE JOB

Getting all the right tools and tech to make your online business a success is a necessary part of this gig. It's also the #1 reason people tend to drop off and quit, because they didn't properly set their expectations to focus on learning these new skills and tools.

There's a significant learning curve here. But the good news is, literally anyone can learn how to use these tools to accelerate your business growth and simplify how you serve your clients.

I've designed this Phase to give you a focal point. So instead of wandering around the internet for 4 hours a day trying to "do research" and figure out which tech or tool is the "best" one to use, you can get what you need immediately and start growing!

I live by a principle in my business, and it's the reason I've been able to move forward so quickly: As soon as it's 70% perfect or better, just roll with it and move forward. And that applies here in this Phase as well.

Could there be some wacky new piece of software out there right now that is incrementally better than the recommendations I'm going to make for you? Yup! But I just don't care, and neither should you. Pick the tools that get the job done and then get to work! You'll discover all the extra little nuances along the way.

You've probably heard of Roger Bannister, the first guy to ever break the infamous 4-minute mile. Do a quick Google search right now for "Roger Bannister's shoes" and take a look at those things! He wasn't waiting around for Nike to be founded and then invent the "best" running shoe. He just dove in with what he had and made history.

And now it's your turn. I'm gonna show you what you need to dive in right now and make history.

CHAPTER 10
EVERYTHING YOU NEED TO GROW

Funny enough, the questions I get most often from new-comers to the online coaching space is always something like, "well which software is the best for _____." And you can insert e-mail, website building, organization, funnels, webinar, video conference, and on and on and on.

Now, since you've been through Phases 1 - 3 already, you know that the best place to start is with designing an actual offer that you can sell before you even need to worry about the tech involved with growing your business.

But eventually you will get to a point where you've enrolled a few clients, money is flowing, and you can turn your attention to some additional tools to optimize your business even further.

In this chapter, I'm going to break down the purposes for which you need these tools in the first place so you start to think critically about which tech you need at which point of growth.

Because using nothing won't get you far, but trying to learn 17 new softwares all at once will just lead to overwhelm.

SIMPLIFIED ORGANIZATION

The ability to organize all the details of each day is the cornerstone of successfully implementing your vision and living out your mission.

One thought that we'll come back to again and again as we move through this Phase is that you must start using systems before you actually need them so that when you do need them, you'll already have them in place, ready to work for you.

The most basic form of simplified organization to put into play right now is a digital calendar system. Personally, I started with Google Calendar because it's free and very easy to use and integrates well with other softwares further down the road.

Plus, it's easy to use alongside Google Drive, which is also free up to a certain storage limit, and is the other simplified organizational tool I used in the early days (and still use) to systematically organize both client files and program files.

VIDEO HOSTING

If you want to create a dynamic online coaching program, eventually you'll need a way to distribute digital material to your clients. This material will compliment the coaching process that you are guiding them through.

For example, when I sold my first 6-month online coaching program, I had a few videos and fieldwork assignments that accelerated my client's progress.

After each session, I would send them a follow up e-mail with action steps for them to take before our next session. In the e-mail, I always included a link to the video they needed to watch and then a link for the fieldwork assignment they needed to complete. The video I hosted on YouTube with an "Unlisted" link and the fieldwork assignment I hosted on Google Drive with a link to a "View Only" document which they could then click File and Make a Copy to create their own editable version.

Then they would upload their fieldwork assignments to our shared Google Drive Folder for me to review and send feedback. Now, eventually, I started using a powerful tool called Kajabi along with Google Drive, which we'll get to a little later on, but for the sake of getting started right now so you don't keep hesitating and "thinking about" which tool might be the "best" for you, just make that first digital training video and get it uploaded and delivered!

SCREEN RECORDING SOFTWARE

When I first got started, I used a software called Loom to record my screen. There are literally dozens upon dozens of tools that accomplish the same goal: Record what's happening on your screen to distribute as educational content to your clients. The basic version of Loom is free, so rather than poking around for weeks trying to figure out which other one might be slightly different, just use Loom and get moving.

And yeah, if you decide to upgrade down the road to the paid version or some other tool, that's great too. But you gotta act and get started now.

SLIDE CREATION SOFTWARE

If you have Microsoft Office Power Point, stick with that. Otherwise, jump into Google Slides, which is also free at first, and start designing your first training video. Put a nice picture as the background, use a black rectangle overlay, with adjusted opacity, and put some white text over the top. That's it! Don't get fancy with this stuff in the early days.

You don't need a collection of epic slides, each one handcrafted by a professional graphic designer. You can do that later when you're pulling in over $50k/month. For now, just focus on your client. They don't actually care about all that fancy stuff. What they care about is whether or not you can get them the result they are after.

Think of it like this, if you're a financial coach and you're helping a business owner get organized with their finances so they can prioritize expenses and budget properly, then chances are, all you need is a well crafted spreadsheet, and a screen recording of you showing them how to actually fill out that spreadsheet step by step. And if I'm the business owner, I don't need an epic 2-hour video training with super fancy slides all about the history of budgeting. I just need your expertise applied to my specific situation, delivered in a high-impact digital format.

If your client feels lost, confused, or overwhelmed (which is usually why they are looking for a coach in the first place), then less information is actually better! Just give them the next step they need to move forward. I promise, if you'll focus just on your client's needs and their next step, you'll start producing valuable content that actually moves them forward, and they will sing your praises for it!

BUSINESS BANK ACCOUNT

Regardless of what business structure you choose, I highly recommend keeping your personal finances and your business finances separate. This may seem like a "duh Brandon" moment for some of you, but I work with enough people who still think Venmo is a good idea for processing their payments that I have to mention it here.

If you're serious about creating an actual business, and not just creating another job for yourself, then stop whatever you are doing right now and go to your local bank or credit union and open a business account right now.

Then open a Stripe account and a PayPal Business account and you will be ready to take payments from people all over the world.

I can't stress this enough - you can't process payments if you can't process payments! Stop making it difficult for your clients to give you money. Make it as smooth and user friendly as possible.

ALL THE REST

Next up, you need a collection of basic tools to build landing pages, design checkout pages, store and distribute your digital course material, automate delivery, create opt-in forms to build your e-mail list, craft e-mails for mass distribution, build complete marketing campaigns, and eventually create a website.

Now, in the interest of getting started now and not getting lost in the ocean of available software, I'm going to recommend just getting Kajabi. It serves the functions of multiple different softwares and integrates easily into everything else you are doing.

In full disclosure, I am an affiliate partner with Kajabi, but only because I personally use their stuff and because I tried out all the other options out there before choosing one for myself and one that I knew would serve my clients.

Use the link below to sign up for a free 28-day trial of Kajabi.

https://www.brandonehofer.com/kajabi

Then, as soon as you are signed up, shoot me an e-mail at...

brandon@brandonehofer.com

I've got a mini-course that guides you click-by-click through creating your very first lead generation funnel, and it's free for everyone who bought this book and uses the link above to sign up for Kajabi.

In chapter 12 we'll dig more into how to leverage Kajabi to create automations that accelerate your growth, but for now, just get started and get familiar with the platform through that free mini-course so you are ready to take the next steps when it's time.

CHAPTER 11
ELIMINATING UNNECESSARY QUESTIONS

I had to include this short but powerful chapter to give you a friendly slap in the face before you start asking all the questions that will keep you stuck forever.

How do I know you'll start asking questions that will keep you stuck? Because I see it every single day, and the more I operate in this industry, the more examples I encounter of coaches and service providers who have amazing value to serve clients with, but get stuck in useless inner dialogue that keeps them completely stuck.

And the most insidious thing about it is that the questions start with tech stuff, but then compound and bleed into every other area of your business, including your inner motivations and mindset. Remember Chapter 2? It's the foundation, but it's so easy to get caught up in the details of tech and all the available tools that you can actually forget why you're doing this in the first place and slide right back into the Employee Mindset, which is characterized by passivity, inaction, and a "poor me" mentality.

WHICH TOOL IS "BEST?"

This awful question gets its own section because it's the one I hear most often. I've seen people stall their business launch for *years* because they are "doing research" and "my due diligence" to try and figure out what microscopic advantage they might be missing out on by not knowing every detail of every software in existence.

Just stop. Stop right now. You can do all the research you'll ever need in a few hours online, and you'll always come to the same conclusion: I need a tool that provides multiple functions related to building an online business.

Just. Get. Started. Sign up for Kajabi and get moving! And you know what? If you discover one year from now that someone created a new all-in-one platform that is even better, then make the switch! But at least you'll have one year of momentum and profit under your belt.

And yeah, the phase "paralysis by analysis" has become a cliche of sorts. But when you see the actual real life effect of this, it becomes a reality!

And if you have to "do research" for a year so you can find a software that is $20/month less than another one, you're asking the wrong questions! You could've gotten started and sold literally thousands upon thousands of dollars of coaching services and that extra $20/month is now inconsequential. But since you made it an issue, now you're stuck wondering which tool is "best" and which one is "cheapest" and on and on.

I hope you can see the message here loud and clear - stop asking the wrong questions.

What's a better question in this case?

Which tool gives me what I need right now in this moment and will help me move forward to enroll and serve clients.

That's it. That's the question. And the good news is, I've already answered it for you.

And right now, if you're thinking, "I better go read a few more books before I decide though," then you've missed the entire point of this chapter and this book.

I'm here to help you move forward, so you can create a new reality for yourself.

WHAT WILL I PUT IN MY PROGRAM?

This question usually pops up after someone has already designed their program and process from Chapter 6. Then, instead of selling the program, serving clients, and making adjustments as they go, they get caught up wanting to design and create a hundred different program modules before making money with new clients.

It's a dead end road friends. Trust me, I've seen it happen time and time again, even when I warn someone of it during a 1:1 coaching session!

This line of questioning begins with "what will I put in my program?" but it almost always leads down the business killing path of "maybe I need a new ideal client" and "what if no one buys this program?" and "maybe I need to redesign the whole thing" and "maybe I'm not cut out for this type of business."

And then before you know it, you're six months in, you've made no sales and you decide to start all over.

Please, listen very carefully - Once you have built your process from Chapter 6, move forward and sell it. Get clients. Serve clients. Accept the fact that your program isn't perfect and never will be. You'll never get better until you start coaching!

You must commit to your path and persevere when it feels like you've made a "wrong" choice. It was never the "wrong" choice. The only wrong choice in this context is to willfully choose *not* to commit.

So what's a better question?

"What is the *one* thing my client needs today that will help them take another step forward?"

That's it!

When you ask that question, the creative centers of your brain will ignite and you'll discover the exact thing you need to create for your client, or for that prospect you are actively pursuing.

And that will in turn lead to deciding what tech or tool is actually necessary to make that happen.

WHICH TACTIC IS "BEST?"

This question usually exists in a more concrete form, such as "Should I sell high ticket? Low ticket? Memberships? Workshops? Do content creation? Make videos? Sell a tripwire offer? Write a book first? Make a webinar?" And on and on. Each question is really just the same underlying fear - "what if I'm not using the *best* tactic?"

But there is no "best" tactic!

Most online coaches and marketing will try to sell you the idea that their tactic is the best and that you are dysfunctional if you don't have it.

In Phase 5, I'm going to walk you through a *principle* based method that will give you a clear path to launching your business. But make no mistake, it's not a magic formula. It's just what I did to get started, so I have experiential evidence that it works. Are there other people in the history of the internet who have done it differently and also succeeded? Of course!

But why bother getting lost looking for the "best" tactic, when you've got a perfectly viable and successful game plan right here in your hands!

What's the better question here?

"Which available tactic connects me with my perfect client while also generating immediate cash flow?"

Can you see why that's a better question? Now you're simply asking which tactic actually moves your business forward. And yes, in Phase 5 I'm going to answer this question for you so you can start building your business immediately and you don't have to get stuck in the perpetual cycle of wondering which tool is best, and which program modules are best, and which tactic is best.

You'll be able to let go of our human inclination towards immobilizing perfectionistic tendencies, and instead make progress!

Sound good?

CHAPTER 12
ACTION AND MOMENTUM

Now you're moving forward! Even the smallest commitments to decide on the details of your business help you establish momentum to continue getting better and better.

And once you've started making those decisions, especially around tools and tech, then you begin to create space for automation.

Automation will only amplify what is already happening. So, for example, if your organic lead generation funnel doesn't work without automation, then it will just be dysfunctional at a faster rate once you introduce automation.

What that means is, until you've done the work of program creation and then becoming familiar with the tools you'll need to succeed, automation doesn't need to be a concern for you.

But, once you *do* have those foundations in place, it's time to create your very first lead generation funnel. Later on in the chapter, I'll explain how I used Kajabi for this purpose early on as I was generating momentum. But first let's get clear on what a funnel is and why you need one.

On the most basic level, a "funnel" is simply the journey that your prospects go through on their way to becoming your clients. It's the process of someone getting to know you, liking you more and more, and then trusting you enough to pay you to help them.

Think of it this way - even if I wasn't using any fancy funnel building software, I could create a funnel based on an organic call to action post on social media, followed by the delivery of a lead magnet inside of Facebook Messenger, which could just be a link to a Google Document, and then that document could offer a free strategy session via phone or Zoom. And then from that phone call, the sale could be made.

That journey the prospect goes on doesn't have to include fancy funnel building software, as long as the heart of the journey remains.

That's what I mean when I say that automation only amplifies what you already have moving. If my simple funnel of organic post + messenger + lead magnet + book a call actually works, then automations will make the result happen even quicker. On the flip side, if my funnel is broken, then automation creates zero leads faster!

So what's the first step here?

Start with your existing social media presence and become more and more present on that platform. Obviously you know I'll recommend Facebook for this purpose, simply because there are already so many eyeballs on that platform.

Then use that platform to offer something of value to your audience. This could be a simple cheatsheet or a blueprint of some sort. Offer that item of value, the lead magnet, to your existing audience with a compelling call to action post where you ask them to comment if they want the resource.

If they comment, you can follow up in Messenger, deliver the thing they asked for and use that interaction as a way to book a call with them.

This is the same type of process when someone lands on a landing page, sees something being offered, enters their e-mail address, receives the lead magnet via e-mail and then gets a follow up sequence inviting them to book a call.

Either way, it's the same idea at the heart of it - asking your ideal clients to self-identify as an ideal client, and then giving them something useful that helps them take the very first step of their journey with you.

BUILDING THE AUTOMATION

So once you have that process in place, where you are able to attract people to your lead magnet by leveraging just Facebook and some well crafted words, now you're ready to build a more automated version of your funnel using Kajabi.

Here's what you'll end up using...

Landing Page - This is a web-based page that exists and has a unique link. For example, if you go to

https://www.brandonehofer.com/your-first-10-clients

you'll see one of my first landing pages that I built to attract people using my lead magnet "How to Get Your First 10 Online Coaching Clients." Now you can begin sending both organic and paid traffic to this landing page, where people can opt in for the thing you're offering.

Form Builder - This is the form that lives on the landing page that is used to collect information from the prospect. In the above example, the form collects just name and e-mail address because most of the time, people landing on this page don't know me personally yet, and so I don't want to ask for too much information right up front.

Thank You Page - Once you fill out that form, along with an automated e-mail sequence, you also get redirected to a Thank You Page with a short video from me that explains how to get the most value out of the lead magnet that you are about to get delivered to your inbox. This is also your first chance to either invite someone to a call with you, or to join your Facebook Group once you get that set up.

Follow-Up Sequence - Once you submit your info on the form, the automation kicks in and you'll receive a series of e-mails that educates you on building your online business and invites you to respond to the e-mails or book a call with me.

And that's the funnel!

There are hundreds of ways to make this more intricate and introduce new types of funnels as you go, but I wanted to give you the most basic version of your first funnel so you can get started immediately!

The first whole funnel I ever built was on Kajabi because it had every tool I needed in one place - It's my landing page builder, my form builder, my thank you page builder, and my follow up e-mail sequence builder and e-mail delivery system. There are other features too, like a complete course platform and checkout pages, and managing payments from clients, and a few other bells and whistles.

And like I said, the important thing is to just pick one and roll with it. You might have another software you're using, that's cool too. But if you click the link below to get a free 28-day trial of Kajabi, then I'll also send you that funnel builder course, where I walk you click by click through how to build this funnel on your own without hiring an expensive web designer.

https://www.brandonehofer.com/kajabi

What I want to highlight here is that you can get the software for free and learn how to build your first funnel for free and then you also book a strategy call with me for free to help you implement everything.

In other words, you're out of excuses! If you've been thinking about launching this business of yours, then now is the time, and these are the tools to get you there. The original promise of this book is that you can launch your business in less than 30 days, and if you're willing to put in the work, you can absolutely start making money in less than a month.

ONGOING GROWTH

In Chapter 7, we covered the concept of building your tribe, and I gave you the formula for using existing audiences to build your own unique tribe. But now you have the added power of automation!

What can this possibly look like as you grow?

Well, eventually you can introduce a paid traffic source, like Facebook ads, to assist you with this automation. With the right strategy, you can get some serious traction with ad spend as little as $5/day.

And by the way, if the thought of running Facebook ads gives you anxiety, then you need to connect with my friend Laurel. She's got an incredible traffic generation system that she teaches for $7/month. And without exaggeration, other people have paid $1,997 or more for the exact same information and training from other phony gurus. She is just way more generous, so she shares all her knowledge abundantly.

You can connect with her here:

https://www.adcoachingfor7.com

Okay, so once you've got some paid traffic coming to your landing page, you can blend your organic traffic with your paid traffic. Then after they opt in for your lead magnet, your follow up sequence and thank you page guide them to your group and eventually a booked call with you.

Here's a simple example of this principle in action. Someone arrived on my landing page from a paid Facebook ad I had been running. They downloaded my guide on How to Get Your First 10 Online Coaching Clients. Then they got the follow up e-mail sequence which prompted them to join my Facebook Group for more resources. They hung out in the group for about 3 months before messaging me privately to ask if I had any coaching programs to help them take their coaching business online. Long story short, they eventually enrolled!

Does it work out this perfectly every time? No way! Sometimes people lurk in my group for years and chat with me on Facebook

Messenger, and then attend a webinar, and then chat with a past client, and then buy an introductory offer, or a book, or something else. And then after all that they finally book a strategy call and enroll in a full 6-month program.

By this stage, you've already enrolled quite a few clients into your premium offer and you're starting to get a higher volume of leads, but not everyone will have the money or the courage to enroll in your full program. Plus, you only have so many hours in the day, so your 1:1 coaching slots are filling up.

It's time to introduce your Leveraged Offer and your Automated Offer, which we'll cover in Phase 5. Once you turn on your automations and lead flow increases, you want to capture as many of the qualified leads as you can by getting them connected to one of your programs or services.

After that, it's time to optimize for client fulfillment so you can retain more clients for longer and longer terms. And that's when you've truly arrived as a fully fledged online business owner.

Will all of this happen in 30 days? Nope. But I wanted to give you a bigger picture perspective for long term growth. That said, you can absolutely start making money within your first 30 days if you implement all of this, and that energetic shift will get you wondering about how to grow and scale your new business.

So here we GROW!

PHASE 5
THE P.L.A.N. METHOD TO MULTIPLY PROFITS

Now the fun really begins! Adding multiple tiers of service offering is where every online coach or service provider gets to create massive new opportunities for themselves.

I'm sure you've heard other coaches all over the internet talk about volume and scaling and you've thought, yeah that would be great to sell a $59 program to 10,000 people. Or to sell a $997 program to 1000 people. Or maybe both! But those numbers don't happen until you've got a massive audience.

The first 4 Phases of this book are designed to help you get started building your tribe and start making money instead of struggling for years trying to figure things out on your own.

But eventually the day will come when you are making sales to thousands and thousands of raving fan clients, so we need to be ready with a solid program that can handle high volume without costing you more and more of your time.

As we previewed in Chapter 6, the PLAN Method is - Premium Program, Leveraged Program, Automated Program, Navigating the Digital Realm.

You can get the free digital training on the PLAN method here:

https://www.brandonehofer.com/free-training

But for now, let's take a look at how you can apply these principles to your business and make them work for you.

CHAPTER 13
LAYERING VALUE

For me personally, I will never leave behind 1:1 coaching. This is a personal preference. I know there are lots of amateur gurus out there preaching about how you *"must"* move to a group coaching only model and how that's the *only* way to be profitable. It's simply not true. Coaches who push one tactic as the only way rather than helping you apply principles to your business will probably be another whole book that I write one day, but for now suffice it to say that introducing a Leveraged Program into your business doesn't mean you have to let go of any other program that is thriving.

The main paradigm shift here is letting go of the belief that 1:1 is always the best way to serve clients. It very often is, depending on the client's needs, but more often than not, a group coaching experience actually creates a better result for someone.

I had trouble overcoming this belief in the early days. I thought, everyone will want 1:1 because that's what they're paying for.

I hadn't yet completely overcome the session by session mindset (which is really just part of the employee mindset).

But eventually I realized that I was limiting my business and my impact by not embracing different ways of providing value.

And so I recreated my offers, keeping true to my original mission and the outcomes I wanted to deliver, and I made The Online Coach Creator a group coaching experience. By doing this, I now had the capacity for hundreds of clients instead of being limited to 15 at a time.

Plus, at $297/month, the potential for recurring revenue is very nice.

Later on, you'll have some fieldwork based on this chapter that will broaden the scope of what you are providing and challenge you to think more in terms of lasting legacy and impact rather than just how to make a living online.

Now, don't get me wrong, wanting to make a living online and just pay the bills was part of my original motivation to make the leap into the online coaching space, and for many others it's also their primary motivation to launch this type of business.

And it will definitely get you through your first 30 days, and probably keep you inspired and motivated even through your first year or two.

But let's not discount the long game.

Once you shift your mind from "make a living" to "impact the world" you'll start to think in terms of legacy, and you'll start to ask new questions that push you to create programs and fulfillment systems beyond just serving people in a 1:1 capacity.

THE LEVERAGED FULFILLMENT MODEL

One very powerful way to layer even more leverage into your business is to introduce what I call leveraged fulfillment.

What does that mean?

Simply put, you will create systems that allow your clients to continue to grow and make progress even when they are not in a session with you, whether that is a 1:1 or a group session.

The best method I've found to do this is creating structured video training sessions with detailed fieldwork assignments that prompt your client to act on the new training they've just received.

These leveraged fulfillment assets should be short and high impact, focusing on what the client must *do* as a result of the training.

Here's a great example - I had a client who was building a body transformation program, helping people lose weight. He built this incredible digital training series that was going to compliment his coaching service.

But then he beta tested it and the feedback was eye opening. The beta test clients didn't watch any of the training videos because they were very long and very dense. And it was just information. It was the kind of knowledge that any weight loss coach would geek out on. But for the average person, they don't care about all that dense information. They just want to lose the weight and they want their coach to give them the game plan!

So we reworked the digital training modules. We made them super simple and short with actionable items at the end of each module. Plus, we baked in systems of empowerment. Meaning, instead of just giving the client a stagnant meal plan, he created a system to empower them to learn the principles of meal plan creation so they could then act on it and do it themselves!

The point here is, rather than getting stuck in a system where your client consumes massive amounts of information but doesn't actually make any real progress until their sessions with you, instead we create a structured path where they progress even when they're not directly communicating with you. That way, the sessions with you, whether 1:1 or group, can focus on application and implementation.

Let me show you one possibility of how this can play out in real life. When I enrolled my very first coaching client, the primary value delivery was through 1:1 coaching sessions. We would meet each week for a one hour coaching session. Then I would follow up with an e-mail summary and a few action items for her to work on. But that was pretty much it.

As my business grew, I realized that I could add more value to her experience by creating short video training modules on subjects relevant to her experience, so I started making these videos and sending them to her after our sessions so she could prepare her mind for our next session together.

Then I realized that often the sessions fell into aimless wandering because we had to figure out together what the agenda for our session would be. So I developed a pre-session form for her to fill out. Now she was encouraged to think through her situation on her own before we sat down for our session. This helped her become more and more empowered, it saved me the stress of wondering what our session agenda would be, and it saved both of us the first 30 minutes of each session trying to figure out what direction we were headed in.

Then I realized that after each video module, there were some action steps that I wanted my clients to take so we didn't have to use our coaching time on things that could be sorted out ahead of time.

So I developed fieldwork assignments related to each training module. In this way, a client could have a session with me, consume additional training material to prepare for the next session, and then complete a fieldwork assignment on their own time.

This is leveraged because it's less time with me, their coach, but it creates accelerated progress. It would be like someone spending 3 hours per week with their trainer in the gym and losing 10 pounds in a month vs. spending 2 hours the entire month with their weight loss coach and still losing the 10 pounds. Same result, just less time spent in "session" and more time spent acting and moving the needle.

Now, on top of what I just mentioned above, I've also introduced a number of different tools, resources, and templates that allow me to layer even more value into my client's experience, while not sacrificing more of my time to make it happen. It's a true win-win!

Part of the process in Online Coach Creator is helping someone develop their own unique sales and enrollment process, but I provide them detailed scripts and templates and guided fieldwork so they can reference these items as they develop their own. I still end up coaching them through part of this, but their progress is amplified with all the additional material. Plus, not to mention the value they get from the community of other online coaches who all support each other.

The point in all of this is to intentionally create a comprehensive experience for your client, rather than just limiting yourself to coaching sessions. Even if you are charging a flat fee for a full program, as long as you are only utilizing session time to inspire transformation, you are under-serving your client and still stuck in the session-by-session mentality.

And in that case, it's a reflection of your employee mindset. Remember, even if you have a business, the employee mindset can still creep up on you and infect what you're doing on a daily basis. Only by thinking in terms of layered value and big picture client outcomes will you be able to remove the chains of this mindset and become the entrepreneur you are meant to be!

PUTTING IT IN PLAY

In the space below, list as many items of value or experiences of value that you could provide your clients. It's okay if none of these are ready to launch yet. For now, it's okay if they are just dreams in your head. Get creative and imagine your business 1 year from now, when all these systems are active. What will that look like?

List all items of value here...

CHAPTER 14
CREATING STABILITY

Let the fun begin! It's finally time to create your automated offer that will bring in new leads and cash flow on autopilot. Now, to be clear, when I say "automated" I don't mean that it takes no effort, or that you will be raking in "passive" income. I mean that you can set up an offer that is delivered in an automated way so that you can reach more and more people without an additional time cost.

But it does take some effort to set up an offer like this.

And that's the whole point. Put in a concentrated amount of effort and work on the front end, and then let that offer attract leads for you.

Initially, you only need one of these automated offers, but down the road, you can introduce more and more to continue building your audience.

The book you are reading right now is one of my automated offers. For me, the primary intention isn't to make any money, because the intention is to expand my audience, help you get started in your online business, hopefully inspire you along the way, and then to offer you another program, like The Online Coach Creator Group Coaching experience, where you can connect with me up to 3x per week in a coaching session and vibe with other online entrepreneurs who are busy building their businesses as well.

Here's the foundation of it all - Build or create something that requires very minimal time to deliver after the initial work of creating it. It can be anything that helps your ideal client take one small step forward.

You want to give them the feeling of working with you, which should involve progress forward! Even if all you give someone is the belief and confidence that they *can* make a change in their life, that is enough!

Think about it, if you've been struggling to do a thing for years, and someone on the internet finally helps you find clarity and see the path forward, wouldn't you want to immediately connect with that person and let them guide you further down the path?

For example, even if the *only* thing you got out of this book was the realization that you must create your life by design *first* and then create your business based on that - even if that was the only thing you implemented, that would totally be worth the cost of the book. And actually much more!

So, in practical terms, what could your offer look like?

It could be a $47 workshop - if your audience is big enough, you can have dozens or even hundreds of people attend a virtual workshop.

After the initial planning, it will only take you a few hours to deliver that workshop. And if you're playing your cards right, you can run some ads to promote the workshop, and then even if it costs you $47 in ad spend to get someone to show up for the workshop, that's okay, because as long as you have a plan to convert them after the workshop, you are good to go.

See what I mean? It's free leads on autopilot as a way to bring them closer to your Leveraged Offer and your Premium Offer. But if you hadn't built your value ladder from the top down, you wouldn't have a clear path to direct them on.

And believe me, I've seen this happen hundreds of times - a skilled coach thinks that selling a $7/month membership will be their launch strategy. Even if you got 100 clients on month one, that's only $700/month total gross revenue. After you account for minor expenses, you'll be left with hardly anything, and now you have 100 clients to serve!

If you see someone with a highly successful low cost membership program, it's because they have other established offers that were already selling **before** they launched the $7/month program. It doesn't mean you can't create one too, it just means that if that's your only offer, you are headed for huge disappointment in the very near future.

Speaking of low cost memberships, that is another model that does indeed work for your automated offer. There are many ways to organize this type of thing, and I don't want to get too lost in the weeds on the exact delivery strategy, but one great example of this in action is my friend Laurel who I mentioned in Chapter 12.

She created an incredible community that you pay a very low cost for, and she over delivers on the training and the value. She teaches live in that group weekly and then records those sessions and uploads them to a digital training portal so students can access all the replays. It's a few hours per week of work for her, but she can serve thousands of clients at a time because of how she has automated her delivery.

Here's that link again if you want to see an example of this type of offer in action:

https://www.adcoachingfor7.com

So whether you are hosting a workshop, a low cost entry-level membership, writing a book, creating a $17 mini-course, or whatever else, the idea is the same - over deliver based on the price you charge and make it easy for people to say yes to your offer.

One of my clients in the fitness space created a $37 introductory offer that teaches you how to create your own workout and nutrition plan. The delivery is completely automated.

You might think, wait, isn't he shooting himself in the foot? If he's teaching them everything they need to know for $37, why would anyone upgrade to his $197/month membership or his $3,000 premium offer.

It's a strange phenomenon within human behavior that when you actually give someone the entire strategy and roadmap forward, instead of being less likely to pay you money, they are actually more likely to pay you money. Even though you've just taught them exactly what to do, they still don't want to do it alone.

In effect, your automated offer is a way for someone to test you out, and make sure you are legit before handing over their hard earned dollars.

This book gives you a clear strategy and path to your first 10 online coaching clients and beyond! And you could go implement these strategies on your own to build your business. But for me as your coach, I want to make sure you understand ahead of time what we'll be implementing together, so that when you're ready for some professional guidance and support, you will know exactly what our path will be.

STABILITY THROUGH AUDIENCE GROWTH

Even though audience building starts from day one of your business, as your business grows, so will your audience building strategies.

One reason the automated offer is so vital to the long term growth of your business is because it facilitates a broader spectrum audience growth process.

Eventually your Facebook Profile will max out at 5000 friends, and you'll need to expand well beyond that if you want to spread your influence and impact to more and more people.

And it may seem like a far off dream right now, but one day you'll have so many people applying to work with you 1:1 that you will have to turn some of them away.

That's when things get fun! Because now you're spending a few hours per week serving people in your Leveraged Offer and Automated Offer, and you can really focus in on your Premium clients, all while cultivating and nurturing future Premium clients with your other offers.

So, for the sake of simplicity in this chapter, I'm going to give you one simple fieldwork exercise that will help you start mapping out your Automated Offer.

DESIGNING THE AUTOMATED OFFER

In the space below, write down 3 ideas for *first steps* that your clients take when working with you. Think in terms of beliefs they need to have before they are qualified to work with you. You can even think of it as "Phase Zero" of your predictable process if you like.

List your 3 ideas here:

Next, write down one lesson or truth they need to implement from each of those first steps to actually make it happen. This will serve as a guidepost for you as you develop the content for your automated offer.

List your lessons or truths here:

CHAPTER 15
OPTIMIZING FOR CLIENT RESULTS

When I first got started in online coaching, I had one goal in mind - Freedom. And I'm not talking about the type of freedom where you work 1 hour a day and spend the rest of your time lying around on a beach. I'm talking about the type of freedom where you get to determine your own schedule, work when and where you want, control your earning potential, serve people in a powerful way, and still have some time left over for those relaxing experiences.

And to be perfectly straightforward here, if your desire is to work very little or not at all, then coaching isn't for you. I'm sure there are other business ventures where you can achieve the goal of not working, but this is not one of them.

If you actually have a mission behind what you do, then you will *want* to work at it. It's just that the "work" in that sense is truly exhilarating and won't leave you feeling defeated at the end of the day.

Why do I mention this here as we wrap up our little journey together in the pages of this book? Simple. The final piece of this puzzle is establishing systems to serve your clients. And yeah, client fulfillment systems may not be the sexiest topic, but it is the lifeblood of your business and always will be.

In the early days of online coaching, it takes true commitment and dedication to do some of the tasks that aren't as exciting as the others, but once you get momentum, now the aim of the game is to keep your clients for as long as possible. Not only because it means for profit for you, but it means your clients will ultimately get better and longer lasting results as well.

Now, we could go in depth on this topic and get into some really dense material, but what I'm going to lay out for you here are just the top 3 considerations you need to implement from your very first client enrollment so that you get into the habit of creating systems to help you serve your clients.

CLEAR INSTRUCTIONS AFTER PURCHASE

Even before someone swipes their credit card to complete their purchase and enroll in your service, they are already thinking, "but what happens after I pay for this thing?" So when you are getting close to that moment of decision where they are ready to fully enroll, you can reassure them that you have a structured plan for what happens next in the process.

At this stage, you should have a few things setup.

#1 - An automated or templated e-mail message that they receive right after their order is complete.

If you're using a tool such as Kajabi, or similar, you can automate this piece. As soon as they buy, they'll get an e-mail with instructions on what to do next. For example, it might tell them how to access any logins or passwords for digital training material relevant for their first week in the program. And then it should also have guidance to book their first coaching session with you, as well as any info they need to get access to group coaching, if that's part of your process.

If you are providing a done-for-you digital service as part of your offer, you will also want to include any links that prompt them to fill out the info you need to get started on their project.

Next, they will want to know how to get in touch with you. That will usually be via e-mail, direct message, Voxer, Zoom, phone, or whatever it is. They need to know that you aren't going to abandon them as soon as they enroll.

Other possibilities include a welcome video to explain next steps and help get them ready for their first full session with you.

This leads naturally into the next foundation.

#2 - Let them know exactly what they need to do before they meet for their first session with you.

This piece is the most critical for eliminating buyer's remorse and chargebacks. Typically, the first 72 hours after purchase is the time when a new client is most likely to regret their decision and get a refund through their credit card company. Unless of course, you proactively eliminate that buyer's remorse through an intentional onboarding process.

For example, the progression might look something like this: After they buy, they get the automated e-mail, which gives them access to their training material. The next day, you follow up in messenger asking them for a picture of themselves so you can announce them in the group. You then officially announce their arrival into your program and congratulate them. Then, other clients in the community can welcome them and affirm their decision.

On the second day after they enroll, you can send them a link with an initial questionnaire or checklist to get their mind thinking in terms of the big picture outcomes they desire.

Finally, on the third day after purchase, you remind them to book their first session or send them a note to confirm their first session and tell them how excited you are to help them get rolling.

Now, that's just one possible progression. The idea is to have them actively engaged in their own coaching process so they stay connected. Give them simple tasks that are very easy to accomplish so they feel like they are moving forward a little bit each and every day.

#3 - Confirm completion of all assessments of pre-coaching evaluation forms that must happen before sessions begin.

In my early days as a coach, I didn't have any of these processes in place, so I would enroll someone, and then we'd have our first session the very next day. That was my only defense against buyer's remorse! And yeah, that can work for your first client or two, but it's not a sustainable business model.

So at their first session, we ended up going through some preliminary work and assessments before we could really dig in. After a few of those types of sessions, I realized I could just ask all these questions on a pre-session questionnaire, and give it to them after they enroll.

Then I would review that form before our first session so that we were both prepared.

The result? Clients started experiencing rapidly accelerated growth because of one simple form that I intentionally put into place.

As you prepare this form for your context, you'll have to ask yourself a few questions to help determine what type of content will be most relevant and helpful. Questions such as, what do you need to know about your client's life or business situation before you can fully serve them in the most powerful way? What do they need to think about and reflect on before they are ready for a life changing conversation with you? And what tools do they need to be aware of and leverage before jumping into the coaching process with you.

CLIENT AMPLIFIERS

Okay, now that you've effectively navigated the client onboarding process, we can turn our attention to the pieces of the puzzle that will amplify client results as they continue to work with you through the process.

Remember, the formula here is to ask yourself, does this accelerate my client's result *and* free up more time for me in the long run? If you can't answer yes to both, then you may have to reconsider the system.

One of the coolest differences between an informational product and a transformational coaching program is the delivery and timing of relevant resources. An informational product just throws a bunch of information at the client and pretty much says, "okay, now figure it out on your own," whereas a transformational coaching process patiently helps the client apply *only* what they need in that moment.

For example, if I'm in a coaching session with a client and it becomes apparent that they still haven't completed a necessary first step that will be absolutely critical for their long term success, I'm not going to give them *more* information. Because in that specific situation, more information will actually hurt them because they haven't applied the foundation yet.

Instead, I might instruct them to review Module 6.2 and then send me a Voxer voice note with an update so we can move forward.

Now, if I didn't have Module 6.2 recorded and posted to the digital training platform, then I would have to verbally instruct my clients again and again on the same concepts to help them move forward. Not only would that drive me insane, but it would also be an inefficient use of our valuable coaching time together.

So, in this example, my client gets a better result *and* I save time by not having to repeat myself. It meets both criteria, so it becomes a part of my client fulfillment processes.

Now it's your turn. Ask yourself these questions to evaluate what types of Client Amplifiers will be useful for accelerating results and optimizing for client retention.

Question #1 - What does every single one of my clients need to *know* before achieving each of the sequential milestones in my program process?

For example, I want each and every one of my clients to know and truly believe that remaining a generalist is the most limiting stance they could take as they launch their online coaching business.

Most people believe that they will somehow "limit" themselves by choosing a specific client type or problem to solve.

So instead of me trying to individually teach every single client this truth, I simply made a short digital training about it and now at the next coaching session we can focus on implementing that truth into their business rather than starting from baseline at the coaching session.

Question #2 - What do I want each client to *do* before jumping into their next coaching session.

In my context, there is a part of the process where my clients need to design their program and then bring it to a coaching session for review.

They will make the most progress if they complete the task of designing at least a rough draft of their process *before* getting on a coaching call with me. That way, when we meet, we have some material to work with and they can get actual feedback on their design.

The alternative would be that they show up to the coaching session empty handed and we begin with design on our coaching call. Then we would have to wait until the next session to continue with the process.

Obviously this would be the least efficient and slowest way to get the job done. It would be like someone hiring a personal trainer and only working out on the 2 days a week they meet with their trainer. But if they did one extra workout a week on their own, and then went walking every day, they would accelerate their result *and* get the feeling that they are empowered to take charge of their own health and wellness.

As the coach, you are the guide and support, but you're also there to empower your clients to take responsibility over their own results.

Question #3 - *How* will my client know they are successful?

Once you've established what your client needs to know and do with each phase of your process, you will also need an evaluation metric so you can both decide if they are ready to move on.

The key here is to establish these standards ahead of time, so you can evaluate systematically, which eliminates all the guesswork.

Not only will this create a better result for your client, but now you will expend less effort to deliver that result because you don't have to make a new decision with every single client. You've already decided ahead of time how to know if they are successful at that phase of the process.

NEVER DONE

You're never really *"done"* with client fulfillment systems. There is always something to refine and develop, and always a new way to optimize for retention, referrals, and raving fan clients.

In the interest of keeping it simple, and not giving you too much to chew on right out of the gate, we don't need to get into the nitty gritty of it here.

However, if you are ready to dig in even deeper to client retention, then I highly recommend you get the book "Customers for Life." It's a simple and straightforward model that will help you optimize your new business for the long haul.

My friend Nic Peterson wrote it, and you can grab a copy here:

https://earncustomersforlife.com/

WHAT'S NEXT AND ACTION ITEMS

To put it bluntly, what's next is action! Nothing will build your business faster than the relentless application of the basics. And nothing will kill your business faster than getting caught up in squirrel brain, jumping here and there from one shiny thing to the next, thinking that there is some magical "secret" that you don't know yet.

Fact is, you have all the "secrets" right here in your hand. And they're not secret. Because these are just the tried and true principles of designing and launching a client-centered business that allows you to monetize your expertise through offering personal services.

And I'm here to help you along the way, because let's be honest, you *could* do this alone. But it's exhausting. And the entrepreneurs who go it alone are also the ones who leave themselves open to vulnerabilities and take 5 years to accomplish what they could have achieved in 6 months.

Below you'll find a collection of the additional resources mentioned in this book that are designed to give you ongoing support as you venture out into the unknown.

https://www.brandonehofer.com/free-training

https://www.brandonehofer.com/mastery

https://www.brandonehofer.com/facebook

https://www.brandonehofer.com/43-new-leads

https://www.brandonehofer.com/kajabi

https://www.brandonehofer.com/your-first-10-clients

https://www.adcoachingfor7.com

https://earncustomersforlife.com/

https://www.brandonehofer.com/launch-accelerator

Visit these resources and when you're ready to get even more ongoing support, shoot me an e-mail at brandon@brandonehofer.com We can quickly review where you're at and what your best path forward will be.

To Your Success,
Coach Brandon